First World War
and Army of Occupation
War Diary
France, Belgium and Germany

62 DIVISION
Divisional Troops
310 Brigade Royal Field Artillery
7 January 1917 - 31 August 1919

WO95/3075/1

The Naval & Military Press Ltd
www.nmarchive.com
Published in association with The National Archives

Published by

The Naval & Military Press Ltd

Unit 10 Ridgewood Industrial Park,

Uckfield, East Sussex,

TN22 5QE England

Tel: +44 (0) 1825 749494

www.naval-military-press.com

www.nmarchive.com

This diary has been reprinted in facsimile from the original. Any imperfections are inevitably reproduced and the quality may fall short of modern type and cartographic standards.

© **Crown Copyright**
Images reproduced by permission of The National Archives, London, England, 2015.

Contents

Document type	Place/Title	Date From	Date To
Heading	WO95/3075-1		
Heading	62nd Division 310th Brigade R.F.A. Jan 1917-1919 Aug		
Heading	War Diary of 310th R.F.A. From 7 Jan 1917 To 1 Feb 1917 Volume I		
War Diary	Northampton	07/01/1917	07/01/1917
War Diary	Southampton	07/01/1917	07/01/1917
War Diary	Havre	09/01/1917	09/01/1917
War Diary	Wavans	10/01/1917	23/01/1917
War Diary	Freschvillers	24/01/1917	24/01/1917
War Diary	Vauchelles	27/01/1917	01/02/1917
Heading	War Diary 310 Brigade R.F.A. Volume II From 1st February 1917 To 28th February 1917		
War Diary	Englebelmer	01/02/1917	28/02/1917
Operation(al) Order(s)	310th Field Artillery Brigade Operation Order No.4	18/02/1917	18/02/1917
Operation(al) Order(s)	310th Field Artillery Brigade Operation Order No.6	20/02/1917	20/02/1917
Operation(al) Order(s)	310th Field Artillery Brigade Operation Order No.5	18/02/1917	18/02/1917
Heading	War Diary 310 Brigade R.F.A. Volume III From 1st March 1917 To 31st March 1917		
War Diary	In the Field	01/03/1917	31/03/1917
Heading	War Diary 310 Brigade R.F.A. Volume IV From 1st April 1917 30th April 1917		
War Diary	Mory	02/04/1917	30/04/1917
Heading	War Diary 310th Brigade R.F.A. From 1st May To 31st May Vol 5		
War Diary	Mory	01/05/1917	31/05/1917
Heading	War Diary 310th Brigade R.F.A. Vol VI From 1st June 1917 To 30th June 1917 Vol 6		
War Diary	Noreiul	01/06/1917	30/06/1917
Heading	War Diary of 310th Brigade R.F.A. Volume VII From 1st July 1917 To 31st July 1917		
War Diary	In The Field	01/07/1917	31/07/1917
Heading	War Diary of 310th Brigade R.F.A. Volume VIII From 1st August 1917 To 31st September 1917		
War Diary	In The Field	01/08/1917	30/08/1917
Heading	War Diary of 310th Brigade R.F.A. Volume IX From 1st September 1917 To 30th September 1917		
War Diary	Vraucourt	01/09/1917	30/09/1917
Heading	War Diary of 310th Brigade R.F.A. Volume X From 1st October 1917 To 31st October 1917		
War Diary	In The Field	01/10/1917	29/10/1917
Heading	War Diary of 310th Brigade R.F.A. Volume XI From 1st November 1917 To 30th November 1917		
War Diary	In The Field	01/11/1917	30/11/1917
Heading	War Diary of 310th Brigade R.F.A. Volume XII From 1st December 1917 To 31st December 1917		
War Diary	In The Field	01/12/1917	30/12/1917
Heading	War Diary of 310th Brigade R.F.A. Volume XIII From 1st January 1918 To 31st January 1918		
War Diary	In The Field	06/01/1918	31/01/1918

Heading	War Diary of 310th Brigade R.F.A. Volume XIV From 1st Feb 1918 To 28th Feb 1918		
War Diary	In The Field	05/02/1918	27/02/1918
Heading	62nd Divisional Artillery War Diary 310th Brigade R.F.A. March 1918		
Heading	War Diary of 310th Brigade R.F.A. Volume XIV From 1st March 1918 To 31st March 1918		
War Diary	In The Field	01/03/1918	28/03/1918
Heading	62nd Divisional Artillery War Diary 310th Brigade R.F.A. April 1918		
Heading	War Diary of 310th Brigade R.F.A. From 1st April 1918 To 30th April 1918 Volume 16		
War Diary		01/04/1918	01/05/1918
Heading	War Diary of 310th Brigade R.F.A. Volume XVII From 1st May 1918 To 31st May 1918		
War Diary	In The Field	01/05/1918	29/05/1918
Heading	War Diary of 310th Brigade R.F.A. Volume XIXVIII From 1st June 1918 To 30th June 1918		
War Diary		01/06/1918	30/06/1918
Heading	Divl. Artillery 62nd Division 310th Brigade R.F.A. July 1918		
War Diary		01/07/1918	31/07/1918
Heading	War Diary of 310th Brigade R.F.A. Volume XIX From 1st August 1918 To 31st August 1918		
War Diary	Authie	01/08/1918	20/08/1918
War Diary	Essarts	21/08/1918	21/08/1918
War Diary	Bucquoy	22/08/1918	24/08/1918
War Diary	Albert	23/08/1918	31/08/1918
Heading	War Diary of 310th Brigade R.F.A. Volume XXI From 1st September 1918 To 30th September 1918		
War Diary		01/09/1918	30/09/1918
Heading	War Diary of 310th Brigade R.F.A. Volume XXII From 1st October 1918 To 31st October 1918		
War Diary		01/10/1918	31/10/1918
Heading	War Diary of 310th Brigade R.F.A. Volume XXIII From 1st November 1918 To 30th November 1918		
War Diary		01/11/1918	30/11/1918
Heading	War Diary 310 Bde R.F.A. 1st Dec To 31st Dec 1918 Vol 24		
War Diary		01/12/1918	28/02/1919
Heading	310th Bde R.F.A. War Diary Vol 27		
War Diary		01/03/1919	29/03/1919
War Diary	Gemund	01/05/1919	10/05/1919
War Diary	Vlatten	10/05/1919	26/05/1919
Heading	War Diary of 310 Brigade R.F.A. From 1/6/19 To To 30/6/19		
War Diary	Vlatten	00/06/1919	00/06/1919
Heading	War Diary 310 Bde R.F.A. July 1919 (Volume 4)		
War Diary	Vlatten	10/07/1919	10/07/1919
Heading	War Diary of 310th Bde R.F.A. From Aug 1st 1919 To Aug 31st 1919		
War Diary	Vlatten Germany	01/08/1919	13/08/1919
War Diary	Heytesbury Wiltshire	16/08/1919	31/08/1919
Heading	311 Bde R.F.A. Became 311 Army Field Artillery Bde 1 Army		

Wost/765 (1)

62ND DIVISION

310TH BRIGADE R.F.A.
JAN 1917 - ~~DEC 1918~~
1919 AUG

ORIGINAL   Vol I

SECRET.

War Diary.

316"Bde R.F.A.

from 7. Jan. 1917 to 1. Dec. 1917

VOLUME I

Army Form C. 2118.

WAR DIARY
or
INTELLIGENCE SUMMARY. 310th Brigade R.F.A.
(Erase heading not required.)

Instructions regarding War Diaries and Intelligence Summaries are contained in F.S. Regs., Part II. and the Staff Manual respectively. Title pages will be prepared in manuscript.

Place	Date	Hour	Summary of Events and Information	Remarks and references to Appendices
	Jany 1917			
Northampton	7th	12 noon	Left Northampton by train for Southampton	
Southampton	7th	7.0 pm	Arrived at Southampton. Left Southampton by boat 8.30. pm	
Havre	9th	8.0 a.m	Arrived at Havre, and left by train for Bavans	
Bavans	10th	10.0 pm	Arrived at Bavans	
"	17th	—	One section from each Battery, the Orderly Officer and other ranks from the Headquarters Staff proceeded to the front line for instruction.	
"	19th	"	One section complete from B/311th Battery (2 Officers Lieut. E. W. Stephen and Stephens handerpump joined D/310 E Battery to complete that Battery to 6 a gun Howitzer establishment.	
"	20th	"	Brigade moved from 3rd Army Area, and was billeted at night in Breackwillers	
Breackvilliers	21st	"	Brigade moved to Vandelles — Argoeues	
Vandelles	27th	—	9 Officers and 96 other ranks proceeded to front lines for instruction. ... with return men	
"	Feby 13th		Brigade less D/310 Battery moved to Engle Belmer	

B. M. Simmings
Lt Col

Original

Vol 2

War Diary

310 Brigade R.F.A

Volume II

From 1st February 1917
To   28th February 1917

ORIGINAL

310th BRIGADE RFA

Army Form C. 2118.

WAR DIARY
or
INTELLIGENCE SUMMARY.
(Erase heading not required.)

Place	Date	Hour	Summary of Events and Information	Remarks and references to Appendices
ENGLEBELMER	15th Feb.		A B & E/310 relieved 104th 105th and 106th Batteries R.F.A. and occupied position in Q.22.a.	JM
"	16th Feb.		The Brigade less D/310 successfully carried out an operation under orders of the 32nd Dn Arty. as shown in Operation Order No 7 attached.	JM
"	17th Feb.		D/Battery 310 relieved the 35th How. Batty as follows — One section on the night of 11/12th Feb. and the remaining sections on the night of 12/13th Feb. 31-1 RFA Howitzers joined the Brigade on the 17th.	JM
	20th Feb.		The Brigade received orders and moved into forward position by sections on the nights of 21/22 Feb 22/23 Feb 23/24 Feb & 24th and finally batteries occupied following positions.	
			A/310 — Q.4.a.2.6 C/310 — Q.4.a.6.7	
			B/310 — Q.4.a.6.5 D/310 — Q.4.c.4.8	JM
	22nd Feb		The enemy commenced to evacuate his front posts and o/w several days of inactivity owing to the enemys retirement the Brigade again moved forward as follows — on 27th D/310 moved our gun into forward position R.4.a.	JM
	23rd Feb.			JM

TMBourner

310th BRIGADE RFA

Army Form C. 2118.

WAR DIARY
or
INTELLIGENCE SUMMARY.
(Erase heading not required.)

Place	Date	Hour	Summary of Events and Information	Remarks and references to Appendices
"	28th	26	C/310 moved into forward position into R+b 5.6 and registered all guns on ACHIET-LE-PETIT. A/310 moved into forward position on this day into R3a37, B/310 moved also and took up positions in R3c. D/310 completes their move, and all guns in Brigade were registered. JM	JM
"	14	20	Capt Hawley and two telephonists wirelops on observation run were wounded. The telephonist gunner Lees	
"	"	21	Major Williams surveyed and M. Lambert of C/310 killed also gunner Hogson D/310 wounded on this date	

JM Roman 26.6.1920

Copy No. 5

SECRET.   310TH. FIELD ARTILLERY BRIGADE.

OPERATION ORDER NO.4.   Feb. 18th. 1917

Sheet

1.   With reference to para. 6 of Operation Orders No. 26, 32nd Divisional Artillery, attached, sub-para. (b). Battery zones will be as follows :-

	A.	B.	C.
Zero to Zero plus 7.	R.1.a.30.85 to L.31.c.15.90.	R.1.a.8.5. to R.1.a.30.85.	L.31.c.15.90 to K.36.d.35.80.
Zero plus 7 to Zero plus 13.	R.1.a.65.85 to L.31.c.55.15.	R.1.a.75.60 to R.1.a.65.85.	L.31.c.55.15 to L.31.c.5.3. to L.31.c.3.5.
Zero plus 13 to Zero plus 60.	L.31.d.4.1 to L.31.d.15.45.	R.1.b.27. to L.31.d.4.1.	L.31.d.15.45. to L.31.c.9.8.

N.B.   Times stated are those at which barrages open on each line.

2.   PROPORTION OF AMMUNITION.   (from Zero to Zero + 60') The expenditure of Ammunition will be as follows :-

	Rounds per gun.	H.E.	Shrapnel.
Zero to Zero plus 7.	20	8	12
Zero plus 7 to Zero plus 13	18	6	12
Zero plus 13 to Zero plus 60	47	30	17

These figures are approximate.

3.   All three Batteries will register the old gun pits at R.1.a.6.9.

4.   ACKNOWLEDGE.

Lieut. R.F.A.
Adjutant, 310th Field Artillery Brigade.

Copy No. 1 Retained.
      2 - "A" Battery.
      3 - "B" Battery.
      4 - "C" Battery
      5 - War Diary.

Copy No.

310TH. FIELD ARTILLERY BRIGADE.

OPERATION ORDER NO. 6.

Reference Map 1/10,000 SERRE edition 1.   February 20th. 1917.

1. Batteries will move into their forward positions by sections on the nights of 21/22, 22/23, 23/24. Registration will be carried out by each section on the day following their moves.

2. All Batteries will thoroughly register the ground between the following lines :-
    Northern Line from PENDANT COPSE to MUNDT WERK.
    Southern Line from L.31.d.5.9. to L.32.d.2.8.

3. Arrangements will be made to complete the new positions with ammunition up to 500 rounds per gun, 75% A, 25% AX in the case of 18 pdrs.

4. Completion of move to be reported to this office each night.

                 Lieut. R.F.A.
        Adjutant. 310th Brigade R.F.A.

Copy No. 1. "A" Battery.
       2. "B" Battery.
       3. "C" Battery.
       4. "D" Battery.
       5.)
       6.) Retained.

Copy No. 5

SECRET.

310TH. FIELD ARTILLERY BRIGADE.

OPERATION ORDER NO. 5.

Reference 1/10,000 map 57D.

Feb. 18/17.

1. The right of the 185th. Infantry Brigade 62nd Division will be extended on the night of the 18th/19th February and will take over from 63rd Division up to the point R.7.b.0.0.

2. The front held by the 185th. Infantry Brigade will be covered by Right Group 62nd Divisional Artillery consisting of 310th Brigade R.F.A. and 312th Brigade R.F.A. under the Command of Lieut. Col. F.E.L. BARKER R.F.A.

3. Lieut. Col. BARKER will establish his Headquarters with G.O.C. 185th. Infantry Brigade and will take over Command of the Right Group 62nd Divisional Artillery at 12 noon on the 19th February from Lieut. Col. KINGMAN.

4. The barrage or S.O.S. lines of the Brigade will be as follows:-
   B/310 Battery... L.32.d.0.3. to L.32.c.30.36.
   A/310 Battery... L.32.c.30.36 to L.32.c.0.4 to L.31.d.68.36.
   C/310 Battery... L.31.d.68.36 to L.31.d.0.3.

   D/310 Battery, two guns PUISIEUX TRENCH in L.32.c.
   two guns PUISIEUX ALLEY from 400 yards from its S.W. limit to its junction with PUISIEUX TRENCH.
   two guns PUSH ALLEY from L.31.b.3.0. to within 400 yards of its S. end.

5. ACKNOWLEDGE.

Major R.F.A.
Comdg. 310th Brigade R.F.A.

Copy No. 1. "A" Battery.
       2. "B" Battery.
       3. "C" Battery.
       4. "D" Battery.
       5. War Diary.
       6.)
       7.) Retained.

Original

Vol 3

War Diary

310 Brigade, R.F.A.

Volume III

From 1st March 1917
To 31st March 1917

ORIGINAL

WAR DIARY
or
INTELLIGENCE SUMMARY.
(Erase heading not required.)

Army Form C. 2118.

310 Brigade R.F.A.

Instructions regarding War Diaries and Intelligence Summaries are contained in F.S. Regs., Part II. and the Staff Manual respectively. Title pages will be prepared in manuscript.

Place	Date	Hour	Summary of Events and Information	Remarks and references to Appendices
In field	March 1st		Gr Balmer of D/310 wounded. Since died	JM
	2nd		The following officers arrived and were taken on the strength Lt. G.P. Denier, 2/Lt A.G. Murray + A.C. Murray, J.W. Proctor 2/Lt C. McElroy. 2/Lt H.A. Sabelli wounded.	JM
	3		Dr Botham of A/310 wounded.	JM
			Gr Shafford of C/310 & Br Grundy of B/310 wounded	JM
	4		Lt E.W.+ Jephson and 2/Lt R. Holburn + J.C. McElroy wounded	JM
	5		Capt. Biggs of D/310 wounded killed. Br Akitt of D/310 wounded	JM
	6		2/Lt + E Greenwood arrived and taken on the strength	JM
			14086 Dr Cranmore A/310 wounded	JM
	8		Gr J.H.Cook, Gr Shepherd, Dr Wrekman of A/310 wounded.	JM
	9		Gr Colley A/310 wounded	JM
	11		Gr W Laughton H.Q. staff wounded	JM
			During the period of occupation of these positions at MIRAUMONT wire cutting in front of ACHIET-LE-PETIT was carried out and also there was intermittently brought to bear on	JM

FWBrown Lt Col

ORIGINAL

WAR DIARY
or
INTELLIGENCE SUMMARY.
(Erase heading not required.)

310th BRIGADE R.F.A

Army Form C. 2118.

Instructions regarding War Diaries and Intelligence Summaries are contained in F.S. Regs., Part II. and the Staff Manual respectively. Title pages will be prepared in manuscript.

Place	Date	Hour	Summary of Events and Information	Remarks and references to Appendices
	March			
In fees	10th		on all the approaches north of ACHIET-LE-PETIT	JM
	11th		Major W.R Cockayne was evacuated to ENGLAND	JM
			2/Lt Punchard + 2/Lt Williams arrived and posted to D/310	JM
			Major Williams evacuated.	
	12th		2/Lt Hirst arrived and was taken on the strength posted to A/310.	JM
	13th		2/Lt H.A. Dabelli evacuated	JM
	19th		Enemy retired from his position in ACHIET-LE-PETIT and the Brigade took up defensive positions as follows in front of the village	JM
			A/310 - L 23 a. B/310 - L 24 a. C/310 - L 23 b. D/310 L 23 b	JM
			2/Lt Foster was posted to D/310 from the 62nd D.A.C.	JM
	15th		Capt E.D. Eveleigh arrived from 14 R.H.A. Bn and took command of C/310	JM
	18th		Capt O.S. Woodward was posted to the Brigade from 312 B'de R.F.A and	JM
	20th		took command of A/310.	
	20th		Owing to further retirement of the enemy the B'de again took up	JM
			up defensive positions in front of LOGEAST WOOD as follows —	
			A/310- G 2 6 42 B/310 - G 2 6 52, C/310 G 2 d 54, S 9 6 5·2	JM

[signature]

ORIGINAL

310th BRIGADE. R.F.A. Army Form C. 2118.

WAR DIARY
or
INTELLIGENCE SUMMARY.
(Erase heading not required.)

Place	Date	Hour	Summary of Events and Information	Remarks and references to Appendices
In the Field	March 26		A draught of 1 B.S. Major and 8 drivers arrived and taken on the strength of the Brigade.	JM.
	27th		The 310 Bde. moved into action under orders of the 7th D.A. and took up positions – B/310 – B23 d 14. C/310 B16 d 90. D/310 B16 d 54. H.Q. at B21 b 99. B/312 Battery R.F.A. was moved into action under orders of 310 Bde & took up a position in B9d	JM.
	29th		A draught of 1 Sgt & 14 other ranks arrived and these were taken on the strength of the Brigade. The following officers arrived & were taken on the strength – Lt H C Ashley. 2Lt K A Hatter. 2Lt A de M Loran. 2Lt F Abraham.	JM.
	31st		The position of the Batteries at MIRAUMONT in case of C/310 in open, the other batteries were in semi covered positions during Brigade holding positions at MIRAUMONT. C/Batty had 4 guns knocked out & another gun hit but not disabled. A/310 had 1 gun disabled by a direct hit. D/310 had sights of 1 gun damaged. No officers flak owing to conditions of ground. Heavy work for ammunition transport. All ammunition carried by pack for 1st 6 days.	JM. P.W.Mangin ??

Secret

Vol 4

Original

War Diary

310 Brigade, R.F.A

Volume IV

From 1st April 1917
30th April 1917

ORIGINAL

WAR DIARY
or
INTELLIGENCE SUMMARY
(Erase heading not required.)

310 Brigade R.F.A.

Army Form C. 2118.

Place	Date	Hour	Summary of Events and Information	Remarks and references to Appendices
Mory	2nd		The Brigade took part in the attack on capture of Ecoust	
	3rd		Capt. J. Willy was posted to the Brigade and assumed command of B 310 Battery vice Major L. B. 99.	
	5th		One section from each 18# Battery moved into forward position on C.B. and registered guns on wire at HINENBURG LINE. Commenced wire cutting. 1 O.R. killed and 2 O.R. wounded.	
	6th		Remainder of 18# Batteries moved into forward position in C.B. registered guns on HINBG. LINE, recommenced wire cutting.	
			Capt. J. Willy M/B Ashby A.C. + K.P.B. Reynolds wounded and 2 O.R. killed, also 13 O.R. wounded + 1 O.R. shell shock 1 O.R. died of wounds. 2 O.R. wounded.	
	7th		were cutting on HINBG. LINE continues carried out bombardment of BULLECOURT.	
	8th			
	9th		Our Brigade active on BULLECOURT, HENDECOURT strong points on the HINBG. LINE in accordance with programme.	

S.J. Thin G.E Major RGA
Cmdg 310 Bde RGA

ORIGINAL

WAR DIARY 315th BRIGADE RFA
or
INTELLIGENCE SUMMARY.

Army Form C. 2118.

Place	Date	Hour	Summary of Events and Information	Remarks and references to Appendices
April				
	May 10th		1 OR died of wounds. 3 OR wounded.	JM
	12th		Wire cutting on HINDBG LINE continued, carried out bombardment of BULLECOURT.	JM
	14		Wire cutting continued, & bombardment of BULLECOURT an for programme. also applied an 'erratic' on HENDECOURT. 3 OR wounded	JM
	14th	7.30 p.m.	Carried out 15 minute bombardment of enemy front line & second line trenches. 2 OR wounded	JM
	15		Fired on enemy front support line according to programme bombarded HINDG LINE mid north of BULLECOURT	JM
	16		Bombarded left of BULLECOURT and factory on U.22.b.15.	JM
	15		4 OR wounded + 1 OR shell shock	JM
	17		Bombarded the HINBG. LINE and HENECOURT also fired on hostile OP's at U15.d.05" and U15.d.d1 during afternoon. 2 OR wounded	JM
	18th		Continued shelling of BULLECOURT and fire on enemy back areas and roads tracks on U.22 a.r & U.21a 7 OR wounded	JM

S B Am b L Major RFA
Comdg. 310th Bde RFA

ORIGINAL

Army Form C. 2118.

WAR DIARY
or
INTELLIGENCE SUMMARY

310th BRIGADE RFA

(Erase heading not required.)

Instructions regarding War Diaries and Intelligence Summaries are contained in F. S. Regs., Part II. and the Staff Manual respectively. Title pages will be prepared in manuscript.

Place	Date	Hour	Summary of Events and Information	Remarks and references to Appendices
April May	19th		Shelled DILLECOURT & HENDECOURT. Reparation Ratio fire on wire. 1 OR died of wounds.	—
	21st		Intermittently shelled Tank in V28 B 35. 3 direct hits were observed on it. 1 OR killed, 1 OR wounded. 2 OR shellshock	—
	22		Shelled enemy howitzer battery in V15a when killing out. Good howls observed. Also shelled enemy support trenches & back area. 1 OR wounded.	—
	23rd		Shelled BULLECOURT and also machine gun at V20 a 96.	—
	25		Enemy wire in Brigade zone intermittently sheared. 18cm Howitzers sent out ranshin shells on 11 am 4-30 p.m in accordance with instructions. Wire intermittently shelled. 1 OR wounded.	—
	26		Enemy TM emplacement shelled at V21 a 85 during night. Howitzers engaged an anti-aircraft gun at V22 c 20 55 1 OR wounded.	—

S S Khn Lt &c Major RFA
Cmdg 310th Bge RFA

T2134. Wt. W708—776. 500000. 4/16. Sir J. C. & S.

ORIGINAL

315th BRIGADE RFA Army Form C. 2118.

WAR DIARY
or
INTELLIGENCE SUMMARY.
(Erase heading not required.)

Place	Date	Hour	Summary of Events and Information	Remarks and references to Appendices
	May 27		Joined with 6" How. on organized destruction of MG emplacements in HINDBG-LINE. Fired 144 rounds of smoke shells on enemy's front trenches during which time the Howitzer Battery shelled support line.	JJP
	28		Fired smoke barrage at 2.30 pm according to orders. Howitzer continued to shell MG emplacements in HINDBG-LINE. Assisted in Counter Battery work.	JP
	29		10 R howitzer CB Battery carrying out wire cutting. Enemy's trenches registered by aeroplane observation. Howitzer 'cracked across'	JP
	30		Howitzer assisted in 'smoke'. A barrage put up on infantry on S.O.S. lines at 5am confirmed very effective	JP
	31		How. 17/4/17 two 18-Pr Batteries noted at wagon lines at SAPIGNIES leaving one 18-Pr & one 4.5 How. in the line all the time.	JP

J.S. Vivian C.S.
May 1917

Cmdg 315 Bde RFA

Original

Vol 5

War Diary

310th Brigade R.F.A

From 1st May
To 31st May.

Original.

WAR DIARY
INTELLIGENCE SUMMARY
310th F.A. BRIGADE

Army Form C. 2118.

Place	Date	Hour	Summary of Events and Information	Remarks and references to Appendices
FRANCE SHEET SAPIGNIES CHERISY MORY	May 1st	12 M	The Brigade fired on back areas and were during the night and engaged and disabused a hostile working party on U31b. & put up a light barrage on S.O.S. lines. One O.R. wounded.	JM
"	2nd		Registration carried out during the day, and approaches to BULLECOURT kept under fire during the night. 5 O.R. wounded.	JM
"	3rd		From 3.45 a.m. the bombardment of BULLECOURT was carried out according to operation orders.	
"	4th		Operations were carried out according to orders. 1 O.R. wounded. 310th Bgde Hrs. moved up to MORY COPSE from SAPIGNIES.	JM JM
"	6th		The Bgde shelled enemy lines remaining in a slow rate of fire when to let up an S.O.S. lines for 20 mins. Lieut. H. Spencer handed over from A/310 to 62nd D.A.C. acc. Lieut. K.S. Jones handed over from 62 D.A.C. B/310 as Lieut. H. Spencer.	JM JM
"	7th		Ranges observed were fired throughout the day; Ammunition drawn from D.A.C. dumps at VAULCOURT.	JM

Pulverisation front adjustment fires

WAR DIARY

INTELLIGENCE SUMMARY. 310 F.A BRIGADE.

Army Form C. 2118.

(Erase heading not required.)

Place	Date	Hour	Summary of Events and Information	Remarks and references to Appendices
	May. 7th	-	Major J.H. Liebe assumed command of B/310. 15 Reinforcements arrived, 1 O.R. killed, 4 O.R wounded	Sheet 1
	8th		4.5 Hour maintained steady fire on enemies line trench at BULLECOURT 1 O.R wounded	Sheet 2
	9th		A barrage was put up from 12 noon to 12.20 p.m & from 12.20 to 12.30 p.m. Aeroplane targets received and engaged. 1 O.R killed 2 O.R wounded.	Sheet 3
	10th		Brigade carried out registration. Enemy artillery less active during day.	Sheet 4
	11th		All Guns were re-calibrated on Zero line. A large explosion seen vicinity of C18 c54. One O.R killed 2 O.R wounded.	Sheet 5
	12th		Lieut G H Watson and one O.R wounded	Sheet 6
	13th		Fired on back areas in rear of SOS lines ; an SOS barrage put up from 3.40 to 3.50 am. 1 all guns registered on Zero point during day. 4 O.R wounded.	Sheet 7

Wilbraham Smith
Adjutant 310FA

WAR DIARY

INTELLIGENCE SUMMARY. 310th F.A. BRIGADE.

Army Form C. 2118.

Place	Date	Hour	Summary of Events and Information	Remarks and references to Appendices
"	May 14th		Fired night tasks according to programme, also 2 short SOS barages put down at 10.0 pm and 2.0 am. H.E. 310 B.a. wired from MORY to C.14 central. 4 OR Killed + 5 OR wounded. 2ht CF Roden wounded both A/310 Battries.	HubSe
	15th		Bombaded with gas shells authoyest up slow rate of fire on SOS lines at 3.30 am.	HubSe
"	16		Fire on German Batteries with gas shells and also fired on Factory V22607 + road leading from BULLECOURT to HENDICOURT.	HubSe
	17		Blew up ammunition dump in V15 c 2 2 , 4.5" How from 'crash' at 2.0 am.	HubSe
	18		Lieut N.B.L Casey arrived reported to D/310. am. 2nd Lt Sharpling 2 w.s. posted to A/310 + 2/Lt Witches, O.R. posted to B/310 am. 37 Reinforcements arrived	HubSe
	20th		A Body of enemy reported massing in U23 centre and were effectively engaged. LABRUIE sprinkled with shrapnel. 3 OR gassed 10 R wounded.	HubSe

Humphrey Hurst
Adjutant 310 F.A. Bde.

Army Form C. 2118.

WAR DIARY
INTELLIGENCE SUMMARY.

(Erase heading not required.)

310th F.A. BRIGADE.

Instructions regarding War Diaries and Intelligence Summaries are contained in F. S. Regs., Part II. and the Staff Manual respectively. Title pages will be prepared in manuscript.

Place	Date	Hour	Summary of Events and Information	Remarks and references to Appendices
May	21st		Roads leading into Hendecourt kept under fire - LA BRULLE kept under shrapnel fire continually.	Weather
	22		Fired on S.O.S lines for a few minutes at 9.30 p.m. Fired on enemy post torpets, and also on roads and back areas in the vicinity of RIENCOURT & HENDECOURT. 2/Lieut H. Hatton arrived & posted to D/310 Battery. 1 O.R. wounded.	Weather
	23		Forty remounts arrived - 14 Horses & 26 Mules - 2/Lieut O.G Bennett transferred to Y/62 T.M. Battery vice 2/Lieut H.C.O Jarvis taken on strength of D/310 Battery. Fired on S.O.S lines for about 15 minutes at 8.45 p.m. Usual shelling of back areas & in vicinity of HENDECOURT & RIENCOURT. Capt. E.W.F Jephson slightly wounded and returned to duty. One other rank killed and 3 O. Ranks wounded.	Weather
	24		Fired "Crashes" on HENDECOURT according to programme. Fired on enemy parties and active enemy batteries V.C.9 and H.B.18.	Weather
	25		Usual routine fire carried out.	Weather
	26		LA BRULLE & roads leading to MORDEN TRENCH kept under shrapnel fire.	Weather

Hawksley Lieut
Adjutant for O.C. Bde

T2134. Wt. W708-776. 500000. 4/15. Sir J. C. & S.

Army Form C. 2118.

310 F.A. BRIGADE

WAR DIARY

INTELLIGENCE SUMMARY.
(Erase heading not required.)

Instructions regarding War Diaries and Intelligence Summaries are contained in F. S. Regs., Part II. and the Staff Manual respectively. Title pages will be prepared in manuscript.

Place	Date	Hour	Summary of Events and Information	Remarks and references to Appendices
	May 27		Fire on MORDEN TRENCH in U.23.b.28. Engaged hostile Battery at U.B.18.	Meusa
	28		Brigade Headquarters moved to B.24.c.0.3 during to heavy shelling. Fired "Cool" on HENDECOURT, and carried out usual counterfiring. 2nd Lt. W.K. Hudson reported arrival and posted to C/310. 2nd Lt. Parker transferred to "Q" A.A. Battery.	Meusa
	29		2/Lieut L.C. Gane arrived & posted to D/310 Battery. Reinforcements of 31 signallers arrived. Rifles firing. Snipers in U.24.c. fires on.	Meusa
	30		Fired bursts on Railway Track in U.22.b. according to programme. Carried out short artillery at U.23.a.72. and at direct hit was observed	Meusa
	31		Usual counterfiring carried out. Guns in sniper in U.24.c. Howitzers fired "Chinese Barrage" lasting eight minutes	Meusa

Arthur John Evans
Capt. for O.C. 310

Original.

Vol 6

War Diary.

310th. Brigade R.F.A.

VOL VI

From. 1st. June 1917
To. 30th. June 1917.

Original

WAR DIARY 310 BRIGADE RFA
or
INTELLIGENCE SUMMARY.

Army Form C. 2118.

Place	Date	Hour	Summary of Events and Information	Remarks and references to Appendices
Moved	1st June		The following draught arrived and was taken on the strength of the Brigade. 31 Horses and mules and 31 O.R. Fired on approaches to Rincourt + between 8.10 pm burst fired on sunken Road. V.23.6.1.0	JM
	2nd June		Back areas were shelled during night bursts of fire brought to bear upon sunken roads in V.23.a.6.0 + 28.6.1.0	JM
	3rd June		Fired on back areas during night	JM
	4th June		31 O.R. Wagoner arrived and taken on strength of the Brigade. Traffic in V.17.b fired upon also NOREEN TRENCH 3 O.R. arrived and taken on the strength.	JM
	6th June		Support line U.14.C.9.9. was registered. Howitzers shelled back areas stand special attention to H.Q. at V.24.a.6.8. One English machine not 5 enemy machines and brought one down.	JM
	7th June		Howitzers registered on crossroads in V.23.d. and special targets in V.17.c. V.23.6 + a rate swept + searched.	JM

WAR DIARY
or
INTELLIGENCE SUMMARY.
(Erase heading not required.)

Army Form C. 2118.

310th Brigade RFA

Place	Date	Hour	Summary of Events and Information	Remarks and references to Appendices
Vermelles	9th Jun		2/Lt Barker and 1/Lt Hall arrived and were taken on the strength of the Brigade. Also 110 other Ranks.	JM
"	12th Jun		Brought 40 other ranks posted to Brigade.	JM
"	14th		Fired according to open alert orders. 13 Rounds.	JM
	15		1/Lt J.P. Twin arrived. 1/Lt Garrett arrived. Taken on strength.	JM
	16		A/310 fired in support of operations & 30 rounds on U15c31. B/310 Special task according to op. Order No 10. Fired 505. Metalum at 9.5 p.m. Then 505 on our own front at 9.35 p.m. Then 505 on our own front at 11.30 p.m. Zero hour being 3.10 a.m. the following morning.	JM
	17		Special tasks according to op Order N° 11. Fired on U17635 2/.	JM
	18		1/. OR killed and 3. OR wounded.	JM
	20		Fired on U17a56. Action how each battery began to move up into positions previously reconfied by 92 Brigade.	JM

Matthew Lieut

Army Form C. 2118.

WAR DIARY
or
INTELLIGENCE SUMMARY.

310th BRIGADE RFA

(Erase heading not required.)

Place	Date	Hour	Summary of Events and Information	Remarks and references to Appendices
	20 June		Battery actions	
			H.Q. 310 Moved in forward position Cgb 67 and registered also	JM
			covered front occupied by the 59th Inf. Brigade	
	23 June		Took over from 92nd Bde RFA 20th Division H.Q. at cgd 67	JM
			and the Battery positions at — A/310 — C14d92	
			B/310 — C15d09	
			C/310 — C15d48	
			D/310 — C21a58 (4 guns)	
			D/310 — Cgd53 (2 guns)	
	24 June		Major G.R. Kenning assumed temporary command of the Bde. 1 O.R. wounded.	JM
	25 June		Batteries carried out registration and fired upon fleeting targets.	JM
	27 June		Position for forward action reconnoitred for 15th Battenia @ 10c. Howitzer fire a destructive shoot on enemy trench reported much complete shoot on U23d17 – U23c93. good hostiles observed.	JM

[signature]

WAR DIARY
or
INTELLIGENCE SUMMARY.

(Erase heading not required.)

Army Form C. 2118.

316th BRIGADE RFA

Place	Date	Hour	Summary of Events and Information	Remarks and references to Appendices
	28 June		Battery forward O.P's established in HOBART TRENCH. Registered 4 points on conspicuous points in QUEANT	M
	29 June		Registration carried out and fleeting targets engaged.	M
	30 June		Routine firing	M

Secret

Original

War Diary
of
310th Brigade, R.F.A.

Volume VII

From 1st July 1917
To 31st July 1917

ORIGINAL

WAR DIARY
or
INTELLIGENCE SUMMARY.

310th BRIGADE R.F.A. Army Form C. 2118.

Place	Date	Hour	Summary of Events and Information	Remarks and references to Appendices
In the Field	1/9/17		Normal Day and Night firing. Roving gun zone burst of fire	JM
	3rd		in QUEANT during night.	
			Fired on RIENCOURT and trenches in area. Enemy aircraft	JM
			very active during this day. 6 Enemy planes flew low over our	
			front line trenches. 1 O.R. Killed.	
	4th		Hostile fire was below normal. Considerable enemy aerial	JM
			activity during this day.	
	5th		Hostile fire again below normal. Normal day and night firing	JM
	6th		Registration checked. Enemy fired V30.63.8. Fired with 7th Dn on bn programme	JM
	9th		QUEANT bomb were registered by us and forward positions of	JM
			batteries. LA BRULLE CROSS roads & approaches to QUEANT were	JM
			fired on during night. Also roads and trenches around	
			RIENCOURT & JENN ALLEY. Considerable movement of the enemy	
			in back area.	
	10th		Registration carried out during day. Hostile artillery	JM
			fire active. Fired on Bn programme.	
			K.S.Nichols Lt Col	
			Comdg. 310 Bde RFA	

ORIGINAL WAR DIARY or INTELLIGENCE SUMMARY

310th BRIGADE RFA   Army Form C. 2118.

(Erase heading not required.)

Instructions regarding War Diaries and Intelligence Summaries are contained in F. S. Regs., Part II. and the Staff Manual respectively. Title pages will be prepared in manuscript.

Place	Date	Hour	Summary of Events and Information	Remarks and references to Appendices
Iv/15/A	11th	9/7	Normal day and night firing carried out today. Enemy's artillery active. Movement again marked. 1 OR wounded. 2/Lt RL Pichan wounded	/M
	12th		Enemy aerial activity today was considerable. 5 enemy balloons observed	/M
	13th		2/Lt. Lt. Hudson posted to 34th Army Bde R.F.A.	
			Registration carried out. 1 OR wounded. Another 7th Div. OR /M	/M
	17th		Fired on NORDEN TRENCH according to programme. 1 wound	/M
			Enemy Artillery activity marked during this day	/M
			Lt. Laurie and Lt. Vandepump wounded	
	18th		Normal day and night firing	/M
	19th		Lieut. R. Walker transferred from 62nd D.A.C. and posted to C/310 Bde	/M
			Our Reinforcement arrived.	/M
	14th		Posted to C/310 B" R.F.A.	/M
	15th		Four Reinforcements arrived	/M
	16t		Our Reinforcement arrived	/M

HAB Holm Lt.Col. Comdg. 310 Bde R.F.A.

ORIGINAL WAR DIARY 310th BRIGADE R.F.A. Army Form C. 2118.
or
INTELLIGENCE SUMMARY.

Place	Date	Hour	Summary of Events and Information	Remarks and references to Appendices
July 15th	22/7/19		Engaged fleeting targets in QUEANT and chiese the registration. Assisted 22nd Inf. Bde in carrying out a raid on our immediate left on enemy trenches V31d. P0.1 were found to be unoccupied.	JM
	23.		Enemy aerial activity not so active. B Bombardment carried out according to VI Corps Artillery Programme. Minnin T+V active. 4.0.R recruits	JM
	24.		Major C.A. Ellis reported arrival and posted to B/310. Fired alright according to programme issued.	JM
	25.		Lieut P.H.P. Reynolds arrived and posted to B/310. 40R ammunc. JM Minnin V.IV active. Normal day and night firing	
	26.		Enemy Artillery active on this day. Normal day and night firing	JM
	27.		D/310 carried out a successful shoot on VA25. Hostile aircraft active	JM
	29.		Normal day night shoot	JM
	30.		Craters on RIENCOURT by all Batteries.	JM
	31.		Mounter's fired on Trench Junctions in V30b. F.S/L.G.R. RFA Cunry 310 B.M.	JM

Secret.

Original

Vol 8

War Diary

of

310th Brigade R.F.A.

Volume VIII

From 1st August 1917
To 31st September 1917

ORIGINAL

WAR DIARY
or
INTELLIGENCE SUMMARY.
(Erase heading not required.)

Army Form C. 2118.

310th Brigade R.F.A.

Place	Date	Hour	Summary of Events and Information	Remarks and references to Appendices
In the Field	August 1st	—	18p Batteries fired bursts of fire into V.25.a.c according to Corps programme during night. Normal day firing	JM
" " "	2nd	—	MOULIN SANS SOUCI & CHATEAU WOOD. was engaged during the day also a suspected O.P at V.24.a.6.3 was fired on. Also HENDECOURT — DURY ROAD was fired upon. A Reinforcement of Q.O.R arrived & taken on the strength of the Brigade. Considerable movement observed in an about QUEANT	JM
	3rd		Normal day and night firing according to programme. Hostile fire on this date below normal	JM
	4th		Crash fired on QUEANT, & PRONVILLE by all guns and Howitzers that could be brought to bear, according to 11 Corps programme. Harassing fire brought to bear on enemy's trench system & tracks in rear. Suspected M.G. emplacement & also fired upon	JM
	6th		Fired on front earth tarafil at D.76.c.5.90 stopped party working there. Minnies U fired on Stwwir during day. Considerable Hostile fire on this date & specially on ECOUST and BULLECOURT	JM

B.S. Kerr Lt. Col. R.F.A.

ORIGINAL

310th BRIGADE R.F.A. Army Form C. 2118.

WAR DIARY
or
INTELLIGENCE SUMMARY.
(Erase heading not required.)

Place	Date	Hour	Summary of Events and Information	Remarks and references to Appendices
In the field	Augt. 8th		Enemy Head Quarters in U24 were fired up on according to VI Corps programme. New trench in U23d.05.63 to U23d.50.15 also. OP in house at U29a.6.3 were fired upon. Normal day night firing. Hostile fire on this day marked. Bullecourt shelled. Hostile Aircraft active also	JM
" " "	9th		Normal day and night firing. Minnie V+2 were fired upon during day. Considerable enemy movement observed.	JM
		10d	Considerable enemy arial activity. NORDEN TRENCH was according to VI Corps programme. Also according to VI Corps fired upon by 18 pdr howitzers. Also according to programme D1 (Sewchend Road) was fired upon by 4 18pr. Batteries in this GROUP. Registration carried out. MINNIE V + Z fired upon. Hostile fire normal. Also considerable enemy movement	JM
In the field	7th		engaged. The 7th Division (less artillery) was relieved by the 21st Division.	JM. D.J.Johns Lt R. J.F.A. O.C. R.P.C

ORIGINAL

WAR DIARY
or
INTELLIGENCE SUMMARY.
(Erase heading not required.)

310th BRIGADE RFA Army Form C. 2118.

Place	Date	Hour	Summary of Events and Information	Remarks and references to Appendices
In the Field	12th Augt.		H/Q R.I.Gp & 2nd Div: Artillery: moved to C26.d.2.6 Maintained liason with Infantry Brigade. Fired on Back areas during night according to Gun fable on Cross Roads at V25.c.7.2 V25.d.5 & .0.6. Considerable enemy movement observed earlier day.	JM
" "	13th Augt.		Normal day and night firing. Echo night firing according to VI Corps programme	JM
" "	14th Augt.		Puff of smoke from enquire seen near QUEANT – Enquire seen & direct hits obtained. Normal day firing & night firing according to programme issued.	JM
" "	16th Augt.		Fired on R.E. Dumps at D.in.14. S/a cross roads, CHATEAU WOOD 1 MG at V23.b.55.45. 4.5 Howitzer Battery fired out anti a/c shoot on V.B.4. 20 rds, 10 rds, 20 rds. Concentration fired with gas shell on Dugouts in V24.a.6.3. to V24.a.6.8.35 .18p.hr on V24.a.9.6 to V24.a.76.00. wood from V24.a.72.61 to V24.a.50.15 night firing according to VI Corps programme	JM JM JM JM

S. Khn L. Col Ed R.F.A.

ORIGINAL

310th BRIGADE R.F.A.

Army Form C. 2118.

WAR DIARY
or
INTELLIGENCE SUMMARY.
(Erase heading not required.)

Place	Date	Hour	Summary of Events and Information	Remarks and references to Appendices
Infbut B	Augt 17th		Normal day our night firing according to programme VI Corps	JM
			1pdrs R/Battery fired on enemy trenches + strong post in U22 + 23	JM
" " "	" 16th		8 Reinforcement arrived at 5 C.R. & taken on the strength of the Brigade. 11pdrs fired on NEW TRENCH in U23a.	JM
		19th	Normal day firing. Night firing according to VI Corps programme. Hostile aeroplanes active on this date - there driven off by our R.A.	JM
" " "	" 21st		Fired on movement in V13b 5.0. area. Following targets fired on ABBAYE FARM enemy in D11d 47. BIENCOURT CHURCH. MAIN STREET BIENCOURT road or FISH CROSS ROADS. Battery position V8 registered with Balloon observation. Night firing according to VI Corps programme. 4 S.Hows. at Dump + dugouts at U17a 72.53.	JM
	22nd Augt		2nd R. wounded. Major F.D. Forbogh evacuated to England + struck off the strength June 1917.	JM
	23rd		According to VI Corps Programme. fired on enemy posts in U22 during day + bursts of fire during the night.	JM
	24th		Normal day and night firing. 2nd R.A. Knight struck off the strength of the Brigade.	JM
			85 Hn. 6 R.H. & R.H.A.	

T2134. Wt. W708-776. 500000. 4/15. Sir J. C. & S.

ORIGINAL

WAR DIARY
or
INTELLIGENCE SUMMARY.
(Erase heading not required.)

310th BRIGADE RFA   Army Form C. 2118.

Place	Date	Hour	Summary of Events and Information	Remarks and references to Appendices
In the field	25th Aug.		The 7th Divisional Artillery withdrew to their wagon lines. H.Q. 312th Brigade relieved H.Q. 310th. Capt. J.M. Currie posted to D/310. Capt. F.C. Pritchard transferred from D/310 to 38th Bde R.F.A.	JR
" "	26th Sept.		Normal day. Tonight firing according to programme VI Corps. Howitzers fired 150 rounds on Minnen T,U,V. Minnen V was registered with aeroplane observation. Minnen T,U,V were kept under shrapnel fire.	JR
	27th Sept.		Normal day firing. Night firing according to programme. 16.O.R. carried from the D.A.C.	JR
	29th Sept.		1 O.R. posted from 49 K.R.R.D.A.C.	JR
	30th Aug.		Fired on dugouts in & around V25 according to VI Corps programme.	JR

J.J. ??? O.R.
Commanding 310th Brigade R.F.A.

Original

Vol 9

War Diary

of

310th Brigade, R.F.A.

Volume IX

From 1st September 1917
To 30th September 1917

ORIGINAL

WAR DIARY 310th BRIGADE. R.F.A.
or
INTELLIGENCE SUMMARY.

Army Form C. 2118.

Place	Date	Hour	Summary of Events and Information	Remarks and references to Appendices
Mancourt	Sep.	1st	Howitzers completed the bombardment on trench n. V25a night firing according to programme.	JM
	"	3rd	Normal day firing carried out at movement observed and night firing according to 11 Corps programme. Much aerial activity towards the evening. 7 Reinforcements arrived and taken on the strength of the Brigade.	JM
		4th	Registration was carried out otherwise normal day firing. 11 Corps programme continued. One reinforcement arrived. Enemy aeroplanes were active today in the early morning.	JM
		5th	1.O.R. wounded.	JM
		7th	Fired on MORDEN TRENCH and UDP19 x15; VCP15 110 according to V1 Corps programme. Hostile artillery active and also enemy aeroplanes were very active during the day. 2.O.R. wounded.	JM
		8th	Normal day firing tonight, according to programme. 6.P. at U23b74 engaged and OPs observed. 1.O.R. killed Hartleyshaw Capt adj for LtCol	JM

ORIGINAL

WAR DIARY
or
INTELLIGENCE SUMMARY.
(Erase heading not required.)

Army Form C. 2118.

310th Brigade RFA.

Instructions regarding War Diaries and Intelligence Summaries are contained in F.S. Regs., Part II. and the Staff Manual respectively. Title pages will be prepared in manuscript.

Place	Date	Hour	Summary of Events and Information	Remarks and references to Appendices
"	Sept 9th		CHATEAU WOOD shelled & Henderson engaged. Heavy X was also fired upon. Corps programme carried	JM
	11th		Raid carried out on BULLDOG TRENCH. The operation was very successful. Prisoners were brought in and loss inflicted on the enemy. 28 Reinforcements arrived.	JM
	12th		'A' Battery 310 joined 50th Divn Artillery to assist in a new operation. Enemy heavily raided our trenches after a severe bombardment, on 185th Brigade front. Right sector, 2 men own, were missing.	JM
	13th		107 Battery joined this Group Artillery. Light firing according to V Corps programme.	JM
	16th		Howitzers engaged Trench Junction at 0.30 & 6.1 with balloon observation. Light firing according to programme.	JM
		13.	O.R. Reinforcements arrived.	JM
		10.	O.R. Reinforcements arrived.	JM
	17th		Lt. W.S. Jones. evacuated. England.	JM

ORIGINAL

WAR DIARY 310th BRIGADE R.F.A.
or
INTELLIGENCE SUMMARY
(Erase heading not required.)

Army Form C. 2118.

Place	Date	Hour	Summary of Events and Information	Remarks and references to Appendices
	September 19th		Normal day and night firing according to programme.	JM
		Night	1. O.R. wounded. Hostile fire in this marked. Chiefly to counter-battery work. Enemy put up heavy barrage N. of BULLECOURT at 11-25 pm to 11.30 pm and was reported at 4.0 am to 4.5 am also at 4.35 am to 4.40 am. Trench Mortars were active also. Hostile aircraft very active.	JM
	23rd		2. O.R. wounded. Successful shoot by D/310 on Howitzer Battery on enemy T.M's. Also engaged U.B.3 with following hits 2 MOR's 10 x 6Y's, 4 Z's, 9 A's	JM
			4. O.R. wounded & posted to Brigade.	
	24th		11 Corps programme continued shoot carried out with aeroplane, but was not completed owing to engine trouble.	JM
	26th		Concentration shoot on BULLDOG TRENCH.	JM
	28th		Major Batley reports to Brigade on posted to command A/310 vice Major D.S.H. Woodward.	JM
	29		Lieut T.B. Wells posted from A/310 to 162nd D.A.C.	JM

Westerholm
and Partridge

ORIGINAL

WAR DIARY 310th BRIGADE R.F.A.
or
INTELLIGENCE SUMMARY.

Army Form C. 2118.

Place	Date	Hour	Summary of Events and Information	Remarks and references to Appendices
Mancourt	Sep 30th		One other rank posted from 62nd D.A.C., and one other rank posted from Base.	O.K.
"	Sep 28th		From 2pm to about 7pm. 107th Battery position was heavily bombarded at rate of fire reaching a maximum of 8 rounds a minute. Day & Night firing was carried out as usual according to programme.	J.M.
"	Sep 29		Programme for day & night firing carried out. Neutralizing fire, and when a destructive shoot was carried out on T.M.b. located at U.23.d.35.85.	J.M.
"	Sep 30		Usual day & night firing according to programme. Destructive shoot on Mine Crater at C.6.d.5.8. with aeroplane observation. From 3.45pm to 5.5pm B/310 was shelled fairly heavily, and again from 5.45pm to 7.15pm. There were no casualties.	J.M.

Headquarters day to day detail

Original

Vol 10

War Diary

of

310th Brigade, R.F.A.

Volume X

From 1st October 1917
To 31st October 1917

ORIGINAL

WAR DIARY
or
INTELLIGENCE SUMMARY.
(Erase heading not required.)

Army Form C. 2118.

310 Bgr R.F.A.

Instructions regarding War Diaries and Intelligence Summaries are contained in F.S. Regs., Part II. and the Staff Manual respectively. Title pages will be prepared in manuscript.

Place	Date	Hour	Summary of Events and Information	Remarks and references to Appendices
In the Field	Oct 1st		Destruction shoot with 4.5" How Battery carried out on Crater C6d with very successful results. The VI Corps Programme was continued.	JM
	2nd		1 Reinforcement arrived.	JM
			D/310 carried out successful shoot on V.25.6.9.3. with aeroplane observer. Considerable enemy aerial activity today.	
	4th		VI Corps programme carried out. Considerable movement observed within batteries enemy back areas.	JM
	5th		Concentration carried out according to observe le Haie shell fire by 4.5" Hows.	JM
			A. D.S.M Woodward proceeded to 3rd Army Artillery schools as Instructor.	
	7th		107th Battery RFA withdrew from action in accordance with 62DA.I No 75.	JM
	7th		VI Corps programme carried out for night firing.	JM
	10th		Considerable movement observed in back areas of enemy.	JM
	12th		2 Reinforcements arrived and taken on strength of Brigade.	JM
			G.O.C.R.A. 3rd Division arrived and taken command of the 62nd Divisional Artillery	JM

S. Mc Loh
Lieut Col R.F.A
Commanding 310 Brigade R.F.A

ORIGINAL

Army Form C. 2118.

WAR DIARY
or
INTELLIGENCE SUMMARY.

(Erase heading not required.)

Instructions regarding War Diaries and Intelligence Summaries are contained in F. S. Regs., Part II. and the Staff Manual respectively. Title pages will be prepared in manuscript.

Place	Date	Hour	Summary of Events and Information	Remarks and references to Appendices
Infch	12/4/10 cont		Artillery covering front. held by 3rd Division. 30 Reinforts arrived	JM.
	10th		Lieut F.W. Barker posted to 59th Divisional Artillery.	JM.
	13th		VI Corps Programme continues. Also concentration with 4.5"How carried out on NORDEN TRENCH. Enemy aeroplane today.	JM.
	15th		Normal day and night firing (night firing according to VI Corps programme.	JM.
	16th		Gnr. OR Killed and 3. O.R. wounded. B/310.	JM.
	18th		Fired serial No 6 of 9/164 according to programme. Considerable aerial activity.	JM.
	20th		2Lt Davis E.W. posted to Brigade and reported to A/310.	JM.
	21st		10 Reinforcements arrived and posted to B/C.	JM.
	22nd		Lieut R.C. Morris posted to A Battery 310 to B/C. 4.5" How Battery 310/ with aeroplane observation effectively Advanced sections moved into position in WANCOURT and HENINEL being relieved by the 3rd Division. 310 B/c was relieved by 40 KB O.R.M.A. Remaining sections moved into new positions as above.	JM.
	24th			JM.
	28th			JM.

D.S.M.M.h Lieut Col R.F.A
Comdg 31st Brigade R.F.A

T2134. Wt. W708—776. 500000. 4/15. Sir J. C. & S.

ORIGINAL

Army Form C. 2118.

WAR DIARY
or
INTELLIGENCE SUMMARY.
(Erase heading not required.)

Instructions regarding War Diaries and Intelligence Summaries are contained in F. S. Regs., Part II. and the Staff Manual respectively. Title pages will be prepared in manuscript.

Place	Date	Hour	Summary of Events and Information	Remarks and references to Appendices
Inholpich	28th Oct.		62nd Divisional Artillery came under orders of the 51st D.A.	JW
	29th		Registered guns in new positions and also registered SOS lines.	JW
			D/77 How. Battery was tactically under orders of this Bde.	
			H.Q. 310 Bde. moved to N15 d 3.3.	
			A/310 went into action at N29 c 00.75" C/310 were in action at N17 c 7.9	
			B/310 " " " N26 b 3.9 D/310 " " " N25 a 35	JW

S.T. Welch
Lieut Col R.F.A.
Commanding 310 Brigade R.F.A.

Original   <u>62nd Dr</u>

Vol II

War Diary

of

310th Brigade, R.F.A.

Volume XI

From 1st November 1917
To 30th November 1917

ORIGINAL

WAR DIARY
or
INTELLIGENCE SUMMARY. 310 H.B/R.M.A.

Army Form C. 2118.

(Erase heading not required.)

Instructions regarding War Diaries and Intelligence Summaries are contained in F.S. Regs., Part II. and the Staff Manual respectively. Title pages will be prepared in manuscript.

Place	Date	Hour	Summary of Events and Information	Remarks and references to Appendices
Lithefield	Nov. 1st	1 P	Brigade came under orders of the 51st D.A. Fired on enemy movement seen during day also registration was carried out by our Battery D/77 How.	JM
	5th		Battery came under orders of the Brigade. Concentrations by Howitzer Batteries in Group on ST ROMMERS	JM
	6th		QUARRY 18:10 on FACTORY. Majors A.F. Boyle and R.C. Foot proceeded to England to attend courses at Shoeburyness.	JM
	7th		D/77. Battery pulled out of action	JM
	8th		How and 18:00 Fired concentration on enemy's defences according to programme.	JM
	9th		One section of Battery pulled out of action and proceeded to wagon lines at FICHEUX	JM
	10th		Remaining section pulled out of action and proceeded to wagon lines.	JM

St John Lt.
Lt Col. Comdg. 310 B.A.R.M.A

ORIGINAL

WAR DIARY
or
INTELLIGENCE SUMMARY. 310 Bde R.F.A.
(Erase heading not required.)

Army Form C. 2118.

Place	Date	Hour	Summary of Events and Information	Remarks and references to Appendices
Lahufield	11th		Brigade proceeded to aerodrome camp at BOIRY-ST-MARTIN	J.M.
	12th		Guns taken into workshops at BAPAUME for overhauling	J.M.
			Brigade marched during evening from BOIRY-ST-MARTIN by road to BOULENCOURT VIA ACHIET-LE-GRAND. Guns were withdrawn from workshops.	J.M.
	13th		Brigade proceeded to BARRASTRE from BOULENCOURT.	J.M.
	17th		C/310 moved into position at HAVRINCOURT WOOD	J.M.
	18th		Remainder of Brigade moved up into position at HAVRINCOURT WOOD	J.M.
	19th		All guns were placed ready for action in allotted positions. 3/2 on our LEFT and 77th and 93rd RFA Bdes on our RIGHT.	J.M.
6.20 am	20th		Zero hour. IN BATTLE. Successfully drove enemy from HINDENBURG LINE	J.M.
12.30 am	20th		B/110 moved forward and took up position East of HAVRINCOURT	J.M.

E.J. Archbold
Cmdg. 310 Bde R.F.A.

ORIGINAL

Army Form C. 2118.

WAR DIARY
or
INTELLIGENCE SUMMARY.
(Erase heading not required.)

310<u>B</u>ᵉ R.F.A.

Place	Date	Hour	Summary of Events and Information	Remarks and references to Appendices
Nov 30th	22nd	—	Moved up to position south of GRAINCOURT. At 10.0 am fired in support of attack on village of BOURLON WOOD came under orders of O.C. 47 Group. 178th RFA Bde	JM
	23rd		Attacked BOURLON Village and BARRAGE to assist 40th Division	JM
	24th to 26th		Fired to assist in shelling enemy counter attacks. 62nd Divisional Inf. came into the line and the Brigade assisted in their attack on BOURLON which had been retaken by the enemy on 26th.	JM JM
	27th			
	28th & 29th		Hd barrages and harassing fire according to the situation	JM
	30th	8.0 h	Heavy counter attack by the enemy along the whole front, beginning at 7.0 am. He was driven back by our Artillery fire and severe casualties caused. Our line is now now 1st line as follows:— F15a3.0 to E15n9.5 to R15c6.7, 6723a6.96 F22n S.S	JM

J.J. Shurlock
Lt. Col. 310 Bᵉ RFA.

T2134. Wt. W708—776. 500000. 4/15. Sir J. C. & S.

Original

Secret

Vol 12

War Diary
of
310th Brigade, R.F.A.

Volume XII

From 1st December 1917
To 31st December 1917

ORIGINAL

Army Form C. 2118.

WAR DIARY
or
INTELLIGENCE SUMMARY.
(Erase heading not required.)

310th BRIGADE R.F.A

Instructions regarding War Diaries and Intelligence Summaries are contained in F. S. Regs., Part II. and the Staff Manual respectively. Title pages will be prepared in manuscript.

Place	Date	Hour	Summary of Events and Information	Remarks and references to Appendices
Battlefield	Dec 1	2pm	Enemy machine guns and movement fired on. also suspected squares in which enemy were reported to be causing considerable number. 1 OR wounded.	JW
	3rd	-	Orders received to reconnoitre rear positions for retirement. 2 OR wounded	
	4th	-	Batteries moved into rear positions. C/310 moved at 6.0 pm on the evening of the 4th and all batteries were in action in their new positions by dawn on the 5th in K.26 + 27, J.33 OR established in K.28.29 and still remained under orders of the LI group. cmd by Lt Col. Parsons.	JW
	5th	-	Responded to SOS calls sent up by our Infantry. 30 R wounded	JW
	7th	-	Registered guns on points in enemy line. 1 OR wounded. Capt Johnson killed.	JW
	8th			
	9th		One OR killed and 4 OR wounded. Enemy dropped bombs from aeroplanes in magazines in HAVRINCOURT WOOD	JW
	11th		Advanced party sent to take over positions which were previously by JW o.c. 310 R.F.A Bde.	Military

ORIGINAL

WAR DIARY 310th BRIGADE R.F.A.

Army Form C. 2118.

Place	Date	Hour	Summary of Events and Information	Remarks and references to Appendices
Lullefield			of 173rd Bde. A Reinforcement arrived posted to the Bde.	
"	12th	—	Battery positions of 173 Bde taken over SOS lines registered and fired on movement observed throughout the day. Light firing carried out on tracks and roads and trenches in the Brigade Zone.	Apx
	15th		Awoke the Bde on our left. fired SOS lines. The attack was not attempted by enemy. 2 Reinforcements	Apx
	17th		Foggy weather and snow. Passed visibility very bad. Light firing carried out on tracks and roads and rear of enemy front line trenches. 150 recruits for battery were fired during night. Programme	
	20th		2/Lt A.T. Cairnsmith and 2/Lt N.G. Wilson posted to A/310. 2/Lt T.J. Starks posted to D/310	Apx
	22nd		7 Reinforcements arrived taken on the strength of B/310	Apx
	27th		The Bde was relieved in this sector by the 24th Bde R.F.A. 6th Division. Relief completed 12.0 am 28th and 310 Bde moved to wagon lives in BAPAUME	Apx

J Mitcall Lt.
OC 310 BdeRFA

ORIGINAL

Army Form C. 2118.

WAR DIARY
or
INTELLIGENCE SUMMARY. 310th BRIGADE R.F.A

(Erase heading not required.)

Instructions regarding War Diaries and Intelligence Summaries are contained in F. S. Regs., Part II. and the Staff Manual respectively. Title pages will be prepared in manuscript.

Place	Date	Hour	Summary of Events and Information	Remarks and references to Appendices
Le Mesnil	28		The Brigade moved by road to COURCELLES-LE-COMTE and was billeted there for one night	J.M.
	29		Moved from COURCELLES-LE-COMTE to AVESNES by road and stayed night	J.M.
	30th		Moved to BERLES. H.Q. at BERLES. D/310 in VANDELICOURT, B/310 in BERLES. C/310 in CAPELLE FERMONT. A/310 in FREVIN CAPELLE.	J.M.
			The following decorations were given to the B.de:	
			H.Q. N. Hea. Military Cross.	
			L/Cpl. Smithenbank. M.M. A/310 Gunner W. Walker M.M.	
			L/Cpl. Clarke M.M. Bdr. to approve M.M.	
			S/Sgt. Stockwell N.M.	
			" Page N.M.	
			D&/310. Cpl. Tatter, Mann. P. MM. C/310. Hosp-Off. Jackson Ba to M.C.	
			Sergt. W. Harrison M.M.	
			Bdr. J. Preston M.M.	
			J Mitchell Lt. Col. 310 B de R.F.A.	J.M.

Original

YA/3/

Confidential
War Diary
of
310th Brigade, R.F.A.

Volume XIII

From 1st January 1918
To 31st January 1918

ORIGINAL

Army Form C. 2118.

WAR DIARY
or
INTELLIGENCE SUMMARY. 3/08[?] RFA
(Erase heading not required.)

Instructions regarding War Diaries and Intelligence Summaries are contained in F. S. Regs., Part II. and the Staff Manual respectively. Title pages will be prepared in manuscript.

Place	Date	Hour	Summary of Events and Information	Remarks and references to Appendices
Suttefield		6:15	28 Reinforcements arrive and were taken on the strength of the Brigade	
	8th		H.Q. On Staff D/310 + B/310 were inspected by G.O.C. 62nd Division at BERLES + decoration distributed. A/310 + C/310 were afterwards inspected at CAPELLE FERMIN.	
		12h	5 Reinforcements arrive and were taken on the strength of the Brigade.	C.A.
		14:15	One section from each battery moved into action behind AVRELLE	C.P.
		15:5	Remainder of Brigade moved into action relieving the 56 D.A.	C.P.
		17:5	The Brigade carried out registration.	C.P.
		18:15	41 Reinforcements arrive at are taken on the strength of the Brigade	C.P.
		20:0	The H.E. Wires fired on a hostile battery at FRESNES which appear to be active	C.P.
	23rd		One reinforcement arrives and is taken on the strength of the Brigade	C.P.
			2nd Lieut C. O. Beaham Jackson arrives and is taken on the strength of the Brigade. Pos. late to D/310.	C.P.
	26th		Major J.F.K. Lockhart arrives and is posted to assume command of A/310.	C.P.
	27th		Three O.R.s arrive and are taken on Brigade strength.	C.P.
	29th		24 O.R.s arrive and are taken on Brigade strength.	C.P.

ORIGINAL

Army Form C. 2118.

310th Bde R.F.A.

WAR DIARY
or
INTELLIGENCE SUMMARY.
(Erase heading not required.)

Place	Date	Hour	Summary of Events and Information	Remarks and references to Appendices
In the field	Jun 9	10.20 pm	Enemy opened fire at a quick rate with T.N's along Brigade Front and to the left. The Brigade fired a concentration in retaliation.	Of
			Battery positions are as follows.	
			Hqrs 310th Brigade H.1.c.8.0. Bty forward guns at H4a.9.1	
			A/ 310th " 326.α.8.4. " Anti tank gun at B29d.9.6	Od
			B/ 310th " B11a.7.4. Bty forward guns at B5d.3.2	
			C/ 310th " H7a.2.2. C bty " " H7d.05.35	
			D/ 310th " B29c.2.0. D bty war position H2b.1.2	Od
			Wagon Lines of whole Brigade are at G.11.c.	
			[signature]	
			Cmdg 310th Bde R.F.A.	

Original

WD 14

Confidential

War Diary

of

310th Brigade R.F.A.

From 1st. Feb. 1918
To. 28th Feb. 1918

VOLUME XIV

Original

WAR DIARY
or
INTELLIGENCE SUMMARY. 310th Bde R.F.A.
(Erase heading not required.)

Army Form C. 2118.

Place	Date	Hour	Summary of Events and Information	Remarks and references to Appendices
In the field	5th Feb		1 O.R. was killed in action.	@ A
In the field	15th		2nd Lieut. J.S. Green arrived and were taken on the strength of the Bde and was posted to B Battery 310 Bde R.F.A.	
	18th		The Brigade was relieved by the 280th Bde 56th Division and proceeded into rest in the MONCHY - BRETON Area	
			A 310 at FREVENT CAPELLE	
			B 310 at BERLES	
			C 310 at CAPELLE FERMENT	
			D 310 at VANDELICOURT	
			HQRS at BETHENCOURT. One O.R. was wounded	@ J
	19th		4 O.R. reinforcements arrived and were taken on Brigade strength	@ S
	20th		4 O.R. reinforcements arrived and were taken on Brigade strength	@ R
	20th		2nd Lieut H.G. Goldsmith arrives and is posted to D/310 Bty.	@ Q
	26th		2nd Lieut P.S. Shepherd arrives and is posted to C/310 Bty.	C. J
	27th		2/Lieut L Lane arrives and is posted to B/310th Battery	C. V

C. Pinchard
2 Lieut. R.F.A.
for O.C 310 Bde R.F.A.

62nd Divisional Artillery

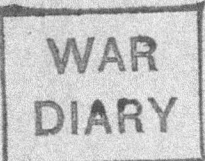

310th BRIGADE R. F. A.

MARCH 1 9 1 8

Original   62 Div

Vol 15

War Diary

of

310th Brigade, R.F.A.

Volume XIV

From 1st March 1918
To 31st March 1918

WAR DIARY
or
INTELLIGENCE SUMMARY.

(Erase heading not required.)

310th Bde R.F.A. March 1918.

Army Form C. 2118.

Place	Date	Hour	Summary of Events and Information	Remarks and references to Appendices
In the field March	1st to 6th		The Brigade is still out in rest	Ad
	6th		The Brigade moved into action relieving the 165th Bde R.F.A. of the 31st Division. Positions were at the following co-ordinates. Sheet 51b	
			Hqrs: B 14 d 2.4	
			A 310 B 9 b 8.5 3 guns	
			B 10 c 2.2 3 guns	
			B 310 B 13 b 4.4 6 guns	
			C 310 B 9 f 5.9 3 guns	
			B 9 b 0.9 3 guns	
			D 310 B 5 c 7.5 2 Hows	
			B 3 d 6.3 2 Hows	
			B 2 c 2.1 2 Hows	
			Wagon lines at A 26 c	Ad

B.M.M.h

WAR DIARY
or
INTELLIGENCE SUMMARY.
(Erase heading not required.)

Army Form C. 2118.

J 10 Bde R.F.A.

Place	Date	Hour	Summary of Events and Information	Remarks and references to Appendices
In the field	March 23rd		Ten reinforcements arrive and were taken on the strength of the Brigade	
	23rd March	Four " " " " " " " " " " " " " " " "		
			2nd Lieut: H.G. Goldsmith was slightly wounded	Cd.
	March 23		The Brigade was relieved by the J2 Bde. and pulled out into the wagon lines	Cd.
	March 24	At 4 am	the Brigade marched from the wagon lines with orders to proceed to AYETTE on the following route. ANZIN. LOUEZ. DAINVILLE. TO WAILLY. FICHEUX. BOIRY Sr RICTRUDE. AYETTE. Here orders were received to proceed to BOCQUOY. When the Brigade had reached F22d sh57D orders arrived that portions of ractiner would be occupied in the vicinity of MONCHY au BOIS. This was done.	Cd. Cd. Cd.

E.J. Hunter

WAR DIARY
or
INTELLIGENCE SUMMARY.

Army Form C. 2118.

310th Bde R F A

Place	Date	Hour	Summary of Events and Information	Remarks and references to Appendices
	March 24		The Brigade remained here for two hours and was again ordered to move to positions west of ESSARTS with wagon lines just east of HANNESCAMPS. The positions occupied were as follows HQRS 310 Bde HANNESCAMPS E.10.C.2.2 Sheet 57D A 310 E7 d r 2 6 guns B 310 E7 d 1.1 6 guns C 310 E7 d 6.5 6 guns D 310 E.18.C.7.7 6 Hows at the Brigade came up acting guns POISIEUX Wagon Lines in E 16 & North of road 2nd Lieut C Game is a wounded	Q.D. Q.D.
	March 27th			
	March 28th		The wagon lines were moved to the eastern edge of HANNESCAMPS	Q.D

62nd Divisional Artillery

WAR DIARY

310th BRIGADE R. F. A.

APRIL 1 9 1 8

Original

Confidential

War Diary

of

310th Brigade R.F.A.

From 1st April 1918
To 30th April 1918

Volume IV 16

WAR DIARY
or
INTELLIGENCE SUMMARY.

Army Form C. 2118.

April 310th Bde R.F.A.

Place	Date	Hour	Summary of Events and Information	Remarks and references to Appendices
April 1st	1st		1 O.R. wounded.	cont
	2nd & 3rd		And very quiet. Our F.O.O's observed for 60 pdrs. and 6" Howrs. from enemy was on line near P.0131.60x.	cont
4th	5th		Four O.R.'s arrived and were taken on the Brigade strength. The enemy started an excessively heavy barrage at 4.45 on all areas to a range of 7000 yards from the front line. All calibres were employed, and H.E. Shrapnel and Gas used. At 5 a.m. we attached ROSSIGNOL WOOD assisted by tanks. The Brigade fired a barrage from 5am to 6.12 a.m. All the wood was captured except the WESTERN edge. The enemy barrage continued up till 11.70 a.m. LIEUT NOWITT and 2 LT SHARPLING were wounded. A/310. 1 O.R. wounded.	cont cont cont cont cont
6th			QMS K A LATTER D/310 wounded. 3 O.R.'s wounded. 4 O.R's wounded.	cont cont

Craig Lt Col RFA
Comg 310 Brigade RFA

WAR DIARY
or
INTELLIGENCE SUMMARY.
(Erase heading not required.)

310 Bde R.F.A

Army Form C. 2118.

Place	Date	Hour	Summary of Events and Information	Remarks and references to Appendices
April				
	7th		Capt. Powell arrived and was posted to A/310 as battery Captain	OJ
			2 O.Rs from 62 Div. T.Ms arrived and were taken on Brigade strength	OJ
			Major Jephson C/310 was wounded	OJ
			Lt. Van der pump was wounded gas	OJ
			8 O.Rs were wounded. 1 O.R killed	OJ
			At 5am our H.F. Hows fired 200 rounds of B.W.C gas in to LA LOUVIERE FARM. K.10d Sheet 7D.	J.
	10th		Very clear day. Many balloons are flying. The 4 Hows fired 200 rnds B.W.C gas on to LA LOUVIERE K.10d Sheet 7D.	OJ
	12th		Evening alive day with abnormal aerial activity. 10/Hows fired 540 rnds and 4.5 How. 120 rnds fo rig of Jimmy	OJ
	13		Period on enemy forward trenches reported. Many casualties reported. Capt. BERESFORD. R.A.M.C. attached to the Bde was from No 8 Field Hospital and Lt. JONES M.O.R.C American Army arriving	
	14th		Lieut. Lt. Shepherd wounded. 4 O.Rs wounded. 65 Mortars Res Col. R.F.A	
			Capt 310 Brigade R.F.A	

WAR DIARY
or
~~Intelligence~~ Original INTELLIGENCE SUMMARY.
(Erase heading not required.)

Army Form C. 2118.

310th Bde R.F.A.

Place	Date	Hour	Summary of Events and Information	Remarks and references to Appendices
April 1	April 18		Lieut Melby wounded gas 130 R.S. arrive and are taken on bivouac strength. The Brigade moves, taking up position in the following places.	a
			A/310 E.16.d.4.4. B/310 E.22.6.2.9. C/310 E.23.a.2.3. D/310 E.12.a.5.2. Bgn Lines at D.16.d. Rear Wagon Lines at COVIN in J.1.a. H.Q. 90.3.500.1577E, Shef. 57D	
	20		Capt Powell is evacuated to ½ Hospital. Church preparations Friday 5 am to ½ hour. H.O.R.S arrive and were taken on Brigade strength	a
	29th		4 O.R.S arrive as reinforcements and are taken on Bgde strength.	a
	24		4 O.R.s " "	a
	25		H.Q. moves into the CHATEAU de la HAIE J.6.a. The O.S.D. and assumes command of Rt & Lt Group. The Batteries move to positions at the following co-ordinates relieving the 129 Bde R.F.A. A/310 K.7.d.8.6, B/310 K.2.c.2.3, C/310. K.1.a.0.7, D/310 K.7.d.4.2 at All wagon lines move to COVIN J.1. a, 170 R.S. taken and taken on Bde strength by S.Q. 312 Bde R.F.A., 48 to proceed in Trues in AUTHIE, I.16.b.	a
	May 1st			
			S.F. Maylord Lieut Col Bde 310th Bde R.F.A.	
			Cronols 310th Bde R.F.A.	a

Vol 17

Original

Confidential

War Diary

of

310th Brigade, R.F.A.

Volume XVII

From 1st May 1918
To 31st May 1918

ORIGINAL

Army Form C. 2118.

WAR DIARY
or
INTELLIGENCE SUMMARY.
(Erase heading not required.)

310th BRIGADE R.F.A.

Instructions regarding War Diaries and Intelligence Summaries are contained in F. S. Regs., Part II. and the Staff Manual respectively. Title pages will be prepared in manuscript.

Place	Date	Hour	Summary of Events and Information	Remarks and references to Appendices
In the Field	1/5/18	—	HQ 310th Brigade R.F.A. relieved at Iba by HQ 312 Brigade R.F.A. HQ 310 proceed into rest in Authie I.16.d. Major C.A. Eles. R.H.A. arrived and posted to C/310 Battery. 3rd reinforcements arrived.	ed.
			76091 Sergt B.H. Shadling of D/310 awarded to Medaille Militaire. Lieut E.W.T. Jephson R.C. arrived and posted to A/310 as Battery Capt.	ed.
	3/5/18	—	2nd Lieut J.G. Fowler arrived and posted to D/310 Battery.	
	8/5/18	—	3rd reinforcements arrived.	
			HQ 310 Bde. R.H.A. relieved HQ 312 Brigade at Right Coy No Iba.	ed.
	12/5/18		From 9 p.m. to 9.30 p.m. FONCQUEVILLERS was heavily shelled with gas shells. Military Medals awarded to the following to O.R. men for gallantry and devotion to duty during operations which commenced March 25/18 :—	
			02191 Sergt T. Mollest E arto atta A/310 715175 G. Forder C/M B/310	
			177686 Bdr J. Mc Curt. A/310 170024 G. Metcalfe D/310	ed.
			176629 L/Bdr Simpson A/310	
			725526 Gnr Pawsey O. B/310	

Olaud Vivychone Lt. R.A.
Brig Lisut.

ORIGINAL

Army Form C. 2118.

WAR DIARY
or
INTELLIGENCE SUMMARY. 310th BRIGADE. R.F.A.
(Erase heading not required.)

Instructions regarding War Diaries and Intelligence Summaries are contained in F.S. Regs., Part II. and the Staff Manual respectively. Title pages will be prepared in manuscript.

Place	Date	Hour	Summary of Events and Information	Remarks and references to Appendices
In the Field	13/3/16	-	16 Reinforcements arrived	
	14/3/16	-	During the past week no special operations were carried out. Harassing fire was brought to bear on various targets including centres of activity, railways, enemy batteries. The Military Medals awarded to the undermentioned for gallantry and devotion to duty which commences March 29/15:— 115729 Dr G. Fisher D/310. 149519 Gr (A/Cpl) & G Evans D/310. 2/Lieut H. E. Marsden posted to 62nd T.M. 310 Brigade H.Q. relieved by 312 Bde H.Q. and proceeded to AUTHIE. Lieut R Walker posted to "D" Anti-Aircraft Battery. Lieut S. H. Crecy posted to C/310 from "D" Anti-Aircraft Battery. Military Cross awarded to Lieut Ab. Mostony of C/310 for gallantry and devotion to duty during operations which commenced March 29/16.	Q.L. A.L. AUTHIE IE. C.F.
	14/3/16 15/3/16	-		
	18/3/16	-	12 reinforcements arrived. Lieut Ho. E. Stephens arrives and posted to D/310 Bty.	C.F.
	19/3/16	-	Major General A. J. Braithwaite presented decorations after Church Parade.	C.F. Standard List, Divisional R.F.A.

T2134. Wt. W708—776. 500000. 4/15. Sir J. C. & S.

ORIGINAL

Army Form C. 2118.

WAR DIARY
or
INTELLIGENCE SUMMARY.

310th BRIGADE R.F.A

(Erase heading not required.)

Instructions regarding War Diaries and Intelligence Summaries are contained in F. S. Regs., Part II. and the Staff Manual respectively. Title pages will be prepared in manuscript.

Place	Date	Hour	Summary of Events and Information	Remarks and references to Appendices
St Le Quein	26/9/18		10 Reinforcements arrived.	a d
	27/9/18		When HQ 10 Bde arrived and posted to D/310 Bty.	C D
	29/9/18		1 other rank killed and 10 Bnrank wounded by hostile shelling of grazing party.	C d
	29/9/18		310 Brigade HQ relieved by 312 Bde H.Q. H.Q.310 proceeded to HUTHIE. Batteries have still carried out harassing fire nightly and several successful shoots have been carried out by visual communication from to 1st Morry to 12th Morry. Brigade was under the Command of the G.O.C RA 41st D.A. and from H.13 16 to 31st Morry under GOC RA 5th D.A.	e d

Claud Sturgeon
2nd Lieut: R.A.A
H.Q. 310th Bde RFA

Original

V8/18

War Diary

of

310th Brigade R.F.A.

Volume XXVIII

From 1st June 1918
To 30th June 1918

Army Form C. 2118.

WAR DIARY
or
INTELLIGENCE SUMMARY

ORIGINAL

(Erase heading not required.)

Ref Sht 57D

310th Bde R.F.A.

Place	Date	Hour	Summary of Events and Information	Remarks and references to Appendices
	June 13th 1918		All batteries ready wartime and wagon lines are in the same location. D/310 fired a successful ranging on hostile battery LY.17 with balloon observation. 50 mob. Two O.R's arrive as reinforcements and are taken on the strength of the Brigade.	cd.
	June 3rd			c.d.
	June 4th		2 O.R's arrive as reinforcements and are taken on the strength of the Bde.	o.d.
	June 6		2 men O.R's arrive and are taken on Bde strength	o.d.
	June 7		Headquarters move from ROTHIE-TO CHATEAU de la HAYE GOMMECOURT PARK heavily and command Right Group.	c.d.
			shelled until 5 p. Two pits of B/310 was damaged by heavy fire of a 20.1 cm:	c.d.
	June 9.		How fired from MIRAOMONT chicken A siglow. killed D/310 wagon heavily shelling after wounded atour R500	c.d.
	June 10			
	June 12			c.d.
	June 13		inds. 10 O.Rs arrive and are taken on Bde strength A/310 engaged KX1 with balloon observation. One hostile system continued taken. Reply damaged with 77mm. Engaged hostile with system Caville area of battery channel.	c.d. 6.l

ORIGINAL S7D

Army Form C. 2118.

WAR DIARY or INTELLIGENCE SUMMARY

310 Bde RFA

Places	Date	Hour	Summary of Events and Information	Remarks and references to Appendices
	June 1918 August		Assisted in a raid on enemy trenches at K11c & M a box barrage.	c.d.
	June 16		Hostiles fired a balloon shoot on LA LOUVIÈRE FARM	c.d.
	June 17		During night the enemy fired about 50 gas shell in E.20.b at 2.30 am in the early morning.	c.d.
	June 17		260 rnds of 150mm fell in E.28 a & b from 9am - noon. We fired a retaliation shoot on L.19c15.35 at 10.35am at 2.50am we fired Programme M. coses 8.25am	c.d. c.s. c.d.
	June 20		At 1.45am the enemy fired 150 gas shell 77mm in E.27d Two small bombs dropped in K3c.d and K9d at 2. am. 130 rnds of 150 mm bombs fell in K 2.c during afternoon.	c.d. c.d. c.d.
	June 21		D/310 moved to positions at J.12.d.99.00. 5 guns. Gun store moved	c.d.
	June 24		B/310 moved back to J.5 & 6.	c.d.

CWWilliams

Army Form C. 2118.

ORIGINAL

WAR DIARY
or
INTELLIGENCE SUMMARY
(Erase heading not required.)

Ref Sheet 57D   310 Bde R.F.A.

Instructions regarding War Diaries and Intelligence Summaries are contained in F.S. Regs., Part II. and the Staff Manual respectively. Title Pages will be prepared in manuscript.

Place	Date	Hour	Summary of Events and Information	Remarks and references to Appendices
	June 24th 1918.		1 section (forward) per battery fretted were relieved by the 174 Bde R.F.A. and went to the W.G.M. Louis	C.O.
	June 25		Remaining sections were also relieved and the Brigade marched to SARTON where it became G.H.Q. reserve. Battries were as follows. A and C/310 H12.a.0.7. B/310 in H.17.a.9.3. and D/310 at H.11.c.9.4. 1/9R. signal and no taken in the Bde. Strength	C.O.
	June 26 to June 30.		Brigade commenced on a programme of intensive training	C.O.
	June 30		The Brigade is still at SARTON	C.O.

Ch Mellor
Major

Divl. Artillery

62nd Division.

310th BRIGADE, R. F. A.

JULY, 1918.

Army Form C. 2118.

WAR DIARY
or
INTELLIGENCE SUMMARY

310 Bde R.F.A. Original   July 1918

(Erase heading not required.)

Instructions regarding War Diaries and Intelligence Summaries are contained in F. S. Regs., Part II. and the Staff Manual respectively. Title Pages will be prepared in manuscript.

Place	Date	Hour	Summary of Events and Information	Remarks and references to Appendices
	July 1st to 14th	15th	The Brigade remained at S. PARTON sur AUTHIE during this period continuing intensive training. On the 9th and the 11th the Brigade sports were held. 12 O.R.'s arrived as reinforcements and set taken on. Bde strength. An inspection by the Corps Commander had been arranged. This was postponed owing to heavy rain.	
	15th		On this day the Brigade entrained at DOULLENS one at A & C Batteries which entrained at HONDICOURT and by "strategical train" before 4 am and for unknown destination.	
	16th		At 6 am the Brigade passed through PARIS and arrived at the stations of AREIS sur AUBE and SOMME SONS via CHALONS sur MARNE during the night. The Brigade obtained	
	17th		During the day the Batteries marched to VATRY and remained there the night 17/18. H.Q. marched to POCANCY and remained there the night.	
	18th		All the Batteries arrived at POCANCY. H.Q is in the CHATEAU. The batteries have their wagon lines about the village and their killitchu in the village.	

Army Form C. 2118.

WAR DIARY
or
Original INTELLIGENCE SUMMARY 3/0 Bde R.F.A. July 1918

(Erase heading not required.)

Place	Date	Hour	Summary of Events and Information	Remarks and references to Appendices
July 19	1918		The Brigade received orders at 4 a.m. - to be on the AY - LA MAISONETTE road at 18 noon. The Brigade moved off at 8 a.m. and marched through BURY - PLIVOT - MAREUIL where orders were received - to proceed - to the country between MAREUIL and AVERNAY. The Brigade halted around the FERME BATREAU 2 kilometres south of AVERNAY (Ref CHALONS sheet 70150) and remained there until 1.30 a.m.	
J.C./205			on the following morning. At 6 a.m. the Brigade was in position of assembly along road from CTOI de MONT RIEUL - to ST MARTIN (Revis du Bûcher) and at 10 a.m. went into action at FORÊT de la MONTAGNE de REIMS. H.Q. at ECUEIL FERME the 18 pndr batteries at PATIS D'ECUEIL at 2233 - 2703 D/31 B. at BOIS D'ECUEIL 2240 - 2715 PLUS FILE DE JONCHERY sur VESLE (howitzers)	J.C.

WAR DIARY or INTELLIGENCE SUMMARY

Army Form C. 2118.

Original 3/D Bde R77 July 14. 1918.

Place	Date	Hour	Summary of Events and Information	Remarks and references to Appendices
	July 20.		Lieut P.K. REYNOLDS D/1710 was wounded in the arm and admitted to hospital	Col
	July 20		We fired a barrage to assist 62 DIV infantry attack MARFAUX. The 51st DIV attacked on our left, the 2nd French Colonial Division on our right.	Col
	July 21.		The attack was continued & fighting at 10.30am. The French took BOILLY.	Col
	July 22		3 O.R.s wounded in action July 24. H.O.R.s wounded in action. Lieut STEPHENS of B/1710 wounded in the back and admitted to BOIS du PETIT CHAMP. field hospital.	Col
	July 29th		Attacked and taken by 187 inf. Bde. The Brigade fired from 11am to 1 pm creeping for on barrage + of ARDRE VALLEY - to assist FRENCH attack on BOIS de DIX MISSMM'S.	O.S O.S
	July 26.		2 O.Rs wounded and struck off Rolls — any N — 2 O.R.s Killed in action	Col
	July 27.		3 O.R.s wounded and struck off Rolls — any N	Col
			FERME D'ECDEUIL tow was shelled and hit & H.O. wounded. W.A. Mitchell - Bagnault at 922241 - 2697. 4 O.R.s await reinforcement + was taken in Bouzancourt	Col
	July 28		The Battn. marched - to - d tack in BOIS du PETIT CHAMP a 2216-2714 at 6.30 a.m. La MAISONETTE CRON works 200 m Nue east Faclabout 500 m Nue N of CUITON Infantry Tabs CHADUZY - BLIGNY - BOIS D'ECLIUSE, BOIS du DIX	Col
	July 29		Noname J Cavalry take montagne de BLIGNY	

310 Bde R.F.A.

July 19, 18.

July 29th   AT 12 noon the Brigade received orders - to advance - Two batteries A/310 at once proceeded - to a position 600 metres N.E. of CHAUMUZY ∴R ARDRE and at 1.30 pm had fired 200 rounds - to cover machine gun nests that were hindering the advance of our infantry. C/310 also advanced and took up a position ∴the ARDRE 400 metres NORTH thereof. the afternoon the Brigade was continually firing, I area at trestle batteries located by aeroplanes.

July 29   At 7.30 pm orders were received that 'A + C Brigade would engage out to the wagon lines in wood S. of FERME D'ECUEIL 2/Tr 101 P.m GA. This was done.

July 30   The Brigade marched off if from the wagon Lines and proceeded H.G. and C/310 - to CONDÉ sur MARNE via ST LUMIER, DIZY MAGENTA AY TOURS, CONDÉ A,B, and D batteries continuing to RECY sur VRAUX AIGNY.

July 31   A and B batteries entrained at CHALONS sur MARNE for DOULLENS. C, D and H.G did not entrain.

Vol 20   Original

War Diary

of

310th Brigade, R.F.A.

Volume XX

From 1st August 1918
To 31st August 1918

ORIGINAL

310 Bde RFA
Army Form C. 2118.

WAR DIARY
or
INTELLIGENCE SUMMARY.
(Erase heading not required.)

Instructions regarding War Diaries and Intelligence Summaries are contained in F.S. Regs., Part II. and the Staff Manual respectively. Title pages will be prepared in manuscript.

Place	Date	Hour	Summary of Events and Information	Remarks and references to Appendices
AUTHIE	August 14th		Reinforcements. Aug 6th: 38 OR. 9th: 1 OR. 10th: 1 OR. 11th: 2 OR. 13th: 1 OR. Brigade continue intensive Training. Hd. Qrs AUTHIE. Batteries at COUIN	S.K.E.
"	Aug 15th		Corps Commander IV Corps inspects Brigade	P.A.E. J.A.C.
"	Aug 15th		Brigade receive orders to select Battery positions in the neighbourhood of ESSARTS and 7th got 600 rounds per gun dumped on same. Positions selected: A Battery F.19.a.99.85. Sheet 57D {B " F.13.d.22.15 {C " F.19.A.51.63 {D " F.19.a.87.50	
"	Aug 16th Aug 16th		Reinforcement. 1 OR. Ammunition taken up to "selected positions" by all batteries during the night.	S.K.E.
"	Aug 17th Aug 17th		3 OR. Reinforcements D Battery take guns up to their selected battery position after dusk and leave them under a guard, the remainder of the Personnel of the Bathn being withdrawn to the wagon lines at COUIN. All batteries continue to take up ammunition at night.	J.K. S.K.E.
"	Aug 18th		All batteries continue to take up ammunition after dusk. 1 OR. Reinforcement A & B Batteries take guns up to "selected positions" after dark, with ammunition. A & B Batteries at COUIN All Batteries continue to take up ammunition. Personnel to wagon lines at COUIN All Batteries continue to take up ammunition at night.	J.A.C.
"	Aug 19th		C Battery take guns up to "selected position" after dark during the night.	
	Aug 20th		All batteries complete their compliment of 600 rounds per gun in "new" selected battery positions. Personnel of A,B,& D Batteries move up to new selective gun positions.	

C. Dunbar, Capt. R.M.
for Lt. Col. Comg. 310 Bde RFA

Aug. 310 Bde RFA

ORIGINAL

310 Bde R.F.A.   Army Form C. 2118.

WAR DIARY
or
INTELLIGENCE SUMMARY.
(Erase heading not required.)

Place	Date	Hour	Summary of Events and Information	Remarks and references to Appendices
ESSARTS.	Aug 21		Brigade, working under the orders of 37th Division fires a creeping barrage in support of an attack by 37th Div. on BUCQUOY. Enemy resistance very light. Attack quite successful. Zero hour 4.0 am. P. Group (310 & 312 Bdes) Hd Qrs being at E 16.d.5.5.	
			At midday Portugese come under orders of 63rd Div.	
			During afternoon Bde. fires a creeping barrage in support of attack by 63rd Div. on ACHIET-LE-PETIT. Attack successful.	
BUCQUOY	Aug 22		Bde. now under the orders of 5th Div.	
			During morning batteries move to positions in squares E.9 & 15. Hd Qrs. P. Group to CLIFF TRENCH. Reinforcements in support of attack by 5th Div. on ACHIET-LE-GRAND. 1 Officer and 1 O.R.	M.C.
			Bde. fires creeping barrage in support of attack, but enemy offers greater resistance.	
	Aug 23		IRLES. Zero hour 11.0 am. Attack successful.	M.C.
			Hun a town attacks	
			Brigade came out of action during the evening, marches to BERTRAMCOURT where it bivouacs for night.	M.C.
			Casualties. 1 Officer killed in action.	M.C.
	Aug 24		62nd Div. Arty. now attached to 56th Division.	M.C.
			Bde. marches via BEAUSSART, HEDAUVILLE, BOUZINCOURT, ALBERT & takes up positions as follows. H.Q. W.19.b.3.6.4.5. A. Bty. W.23.d.8.8., B. Bty. W.23.b.75.20., C. Bty. W.2.b.6.3. J. M.E. D.Btty. W.22 Central. 1 Officer Reinforcement. C. Newstead Capt. P.M. for Lt. Col. Cmdg. 310 Bde R.F.A.

ORIGINAL

Army Form C. 2118.

WAR DIARY
or
INTELLIGENCE SUMMARY.
(Erase heading not required.)

Instructions regarding War Diaries and Intelligence Summaries are contained in F. S. Regs., Part II. and the Staff Manual respectively. Title pages will be prepared in manuscript.

Place	Date	Hour	Summary of Events and Information	Remarks and references to Appendices
ALBERT.	25th Aug.		Zero hour 2.30 am. A+B Batteries fire creeping barrage in support of Inf. attack on CONTALMAISON. Successful.	J.M.C.
			D Bty. move forward to N.23. central at dawn.	J.M.C.
			During 15th morning the Bde advances to Bde. Hd. Qrs. X.15.a.9.2.	J.M.C.
			A. Bty. X.14.a.9.1.	
			B. Bty. X.14.b.2.9.	
			C. Bty. X.14.b.7.7.	
			D. Bty. X.14.b.6.6.	
			Wagon Lines X.23 Central. Sheet 57DSE.	
	26th Aug.		Zero hour 4.30 am. Bde. fire creeping barrage in support of attack by 38th Div. on BAZENTIN-LE-GRAND, barrage starting from 1k. west of BAZENTIN-LE-GRAND & moving east to the outskirts of LONGUEVAL. Attack successful.	J.M.C.
			At 6.45 am Bde. bombard HIGH WOOD for half an hour.	J.M.C.
			At 11.0 am C & D Btys. move forward. A+B Btys. follow as soon as C & D are in position.	J.M.C.
			New positions A. Bty. X.10.d.80.88. ⎫	
			B. Bty. X.10.d.99.50. ⎬ Sheet 57DSE	
			C. Bty. X.10.d.82.60. ⎭	
			D. Bty. X.10.c.4.5.	
			Bde. H.Q. move to S.13.d.1.8. (Sheet 57 S.W.)	J.M.C.
			During afternoon Bde. support attack on LONGUEVAL. Inf. enter the village but are forced to withdraw during evening.	J.M.C.

C. Veemehup Capt. R.F.A.
for Lt. Col. Cmdg. JCO Bde. R.F.A.

ORIGINAL

310. Bde. R.F.A.

Army Form C. 2118.

WAR DIARY
or
INTELLIGENCE SUMMARY.
(Erase heading not required.)

Instructions regarding War Diaries and Intelligence Summaries are contained in F. S. Regs., Part II. and the Staff Manual respectively. Title pages will be prepared in manuscript.

Place	Date	Hour	Summary of Events and Information	Remarks and references to Appendices
	26th Aug		At 8.0 pm Bde. fire a preventative barrage on line S.10 central to S.16 central to stop enemy counter attack developing.	J.A.C.
	27 Aug		Zero hour 5.30 am. Bde. fire creeping barrage in support of Inf. attack on LONGUEVAL and DELVILLE WOOD both of which are taken during the morning but are lost again during enemy counter attack in the afternoon. Bde. fire concentrations on LONGUEVAL & DELVILLE WOOD throughout its night. Casualties 7 O.R. wounded.	J.A.C. J.A.C.
	28th Aug		Harassing fire carried out by Bde. throughout the day & night.	J.A.C.
	24th Aug.		Zero hour 5.15 am. Bde. fire creeping barrage from a line running north and south through centre of LONGUEVAL moving east to N.4.5. grid line 500x E. of GINCHY. GINCHY & GUILLEMONT captured during morning. During morning Bde. move forward to the following positions:— Bde. H.Q to S.17.b.4.3. A. Bty. to S.23.b.6.2. 57° S.W. { B. Bty. to S.23.d.3.2. C. Bty. to S.24.a.2.7. D. Bty. to S.23.c.8.4.	J.A.C.

C. Leuchars Capt. RHA
for Lt. Col. Commdg.
300 (?) Bde (?)

ORIGINAL

310 Bde. R.F.A.

Army Form C. 2118.

WAR DIARY
or
INTELLIGENCE SUMMARY.
(Erase heading not required.)

Place	Date	Hour	Summary of Events and Information	Remarks and references to Appendices
	29th Aug.		Zero hour 6.0 p.m. Bde fire creeping barrage over MORVAL from west to east in support of Inft. attack on same. Attack held up by heavy machine gun fire and proved a failure.	A.E.
	30th Aug.		Zero hour 5.0 a.m. Bde fire creeping barrage starting from road running south from eastern end of Morval (T.11.c.4.0) to T.D central & working east to N.& S. grid line T.12.18 to T.18 central. Inft. lose direction; hostile machine gun fire very heavy; MORVAL not taken. During afternoon A & C Btys move forward to following locations:- A Bty. T.13.c.20.75 C Bty. T.19.a.6.7.	
	31st Aug.		During morning B & D Btys move forward to:- B Bty. T.14.c.4.4 D Bty, { 2 Hows. T.13.b.6.3 GINCHY { 2 Hows. T.13.d.9.0. 4.0 p.m. to 6.0 p.m. Bde. in conjunction with remainder of 38 Div Arty. + V.C.H.A bombard area between MORVAL and SAILLY-SAILLISEL with a view to making enemy believe that an attack is in progress, and also to prepare the way for the attack to take place morning of Sept 1st. C. Luncher? Capt. RFA for Lt. Col. Aug. 310 D.E. RFA	

Original

Vol 21

War Diary

of

310th Brigade, R.F.A.

Volume ~~IX~~
XXI

From 1st September 1918
To 30th September 1918

Original

310 Bde R.F.A.

Army Form C.2118.

WAR DIARY
or
INTELLIGENCE SUMMARY.
(Erase heading not required.)

Instructions regarding War Diaries and Intelligence Summaries are contained in F.S. Regs., Part II. and the Staff Manual respectively. Title pages will be prepared in manuscript.

Place	Date	Hour	Summary of Events and Information	Remarks and references to Appendices
	1st Sept	16/18	Ref. Sheet. Bde. move forward & take up positions in U.15 & 16 & fire creeping barrage in support of Inf. attack on U.15 & 16.	M.E.
	2nd Sept.	"	No move.	M.E.
	3rd Sept.		H.Q. 310 Bde move to T.17.d.5.65.	M.E.
	4th Sept.		Bde. HQ move to U.14.c.7.1. A & C Btys move to positions in U.19.9.15. B & D Btys to U.12.d.	M.E.
	6th Sept.		Bde. HQ. move to U.23. Central, Btys. to V.14.a.20.	M.E.
	7th Sept.		Bde. relieved by 72nd Bde. R.F.A. at 6.0 pm & withdrew to LE TRANSLOY.	M.E.
	8th Sept.	10.0 am	Bde. marched to GOMIECOURT.	M.E.
	9th Sept.		Bde. march to BEUGNY. Lt Col. (D) SHERLOCK D.S.O. took over command of the 'Left Group' consisting of the 310, 312 & 76 Bdes R.F.A. Handing M.E. over 187 Inf. Bde. Major G. A. EELES D.S.O. took over the command of the 310 Bde R.F.A.	D.A.C.

Original

310 Bde. R.F.A.

Army Form C. 2118.

WAR DIARY
or
INTELLIGENCE SUMMARY.
(Erase heading not required.)

Instructions regarding War Diaries and Intelligence Summaries are contained in F. S. Regs., Part II. and the Staff Manual respectively. Title pages will be prepared in manuscript.

Place	Date	Hour	Summary of Events and Information	Remarks and references to Appendices
	10th Sept 1918		Bde. came into action in T.6.a.& b. (Ref. Sheet. 57c S.W.)	M.E.
	11th Sept 1918		Bde H.Q. established at T.6.b.6.5.7.	M.E.
	12th Sept 1918.		Bde. fire creeping barrage in support of attack on HAVRINCOURT. Zero hour being at 5.25 am. Attack successful.	M.E.
			S.O.S. received at 7.7 p.m. & answered by all batteries. No hostile attack developed.	M.E.
	14th Sept. 1918		Zero hour 5.20 am. Bde. fire creeping barrage in support of attack on trenches east of HAVRINCOURT WOOD. Attack successful.	M.E.
	15th Sept. 1918		Counter Preparation fired at 5.20 am.	M.E.
			S.O.S. fired on by all batteries at 6.0 p.m. No hostile attack developed.	M.E.
	16th Sept 1918		Counter Preparation fired at 5.20 am.	M.E.
	18th Sept 1918		During early morning Bde. fired smoke barrage in support of an attack by 1st Div on our right flank.	M.E.
	19th/20th Sept to 25th		Heavy harassing fire carried out by Bde.	M.E.
	26th Sept 1918		Btys. move to Q.2.c. Shelock Group move to BOGGART'S HOLE behind HAVRINCOURT.	M.E.

Original

310 Bde. R.F.A.

Army Form C. 2118.

WAR DIARY
or
INTELLIGENCE SUMMARY.

(Erase heading not required.)

Instructions regarding War Diaries and Intelligence Summaries are contained in F. S. Regs. Part II. and the Staff Manual respectively. Title pages will be prepared in manuscript.

Place	Date	Hour	Summary of Events and Information	Remarks and references to Appendices
	27th Sept. 1918	5.20 am	Zero hour 5.20 am. Bde. fire creeping barrage in support of attack on RIBECOURT. Attack successful.	S.A.E.
	28th Sept 1918		During morning batteries move to K.30.b. (Sheet 57c N.E.) Bde. H.Q. move to K.29.d.10.30. Sherlock Group to L.19.c.35.50. Bde fire creeping barrage in support of attack on country S. of RIBECOURT. L.26.	S.A.E. S.A.E.
	29th Sept 1918	7.30 am	Zero hour 7.30 am. Bde. fire barrage in support of attack on MESNIÈRES & trench system beyond. Attack successful. At midday Bde. move to L.28.d. Bde H.Q. L.34.b.1.8.	S.A.E.
	30th Sept 1918		One Section of B.Bty. under Lt. HESS. M.E. moves to G.25.d.7.2. (Sheet 57B N.W.)	S.A.E.

Secret. — Original

No 2

War Diary
of
310th Brigade, R.F.A.

Volume XXII

From 1st October 1918
To 31st October 1918

WAR DIARY
or
INTELLIGENCE SUMMARY.

Army Form C. 2118.

310 Bde. R.F.A.

Place	Date	Hour	Summary of Events and Information	Remarks and references to Appendices
	Oct 1st 1918		Zero hour 6.0 a.m. Bde fired a creeping barrage in support of an attack upon RUMILLY. Most of the village was taken. Zero hour 6.0 p.m. Bde fired creeping barrage in support of an attack upon that part of RUMILLY that still remained in the enemy's hands. Fired 9 mm rounds I.O.R.	M.C. M.C.
	Oct 2nd-3rd 1918		No move on part of Bde. Lt N. HESS M.C. took two detachments of gunners up to MASNIÈRES & harassed back areas with German 77 mm guns + 150 mm Howitzer.	M.C. M.C.
	Oct 4th 1918		Batteries move forward to eastern outskirts of MASNIÈRES (G27 a+c) keeping N. of the canal at St QUENTIN during the morning. 5.30 pm orders are received to withdraw immediately to former positions in L.28. C Bty leave one section behind under the charge of Lt A.C. MURRAY M.C. to act as anti-tank defence	M.C.

Army Form C. 2118.

WAR DIARY
or
INTELLIGENCE SUMMARY.

310 Bde. R.F.A.

(Erase heading not required.)

Instructions regarding War Diaries and Intelligence Summaries are contained in F.S. Regs., Part II. and the Staff Manual respectively. Title pages will be prepared in manuscript.

Place	Date	Hour	Summary of Events and Information	Remarks and references to Appendices
	5th Oct 1918		Batteries move forward to positions in L.36. S.E. of MASNIÈRES	M.E.
	6th Oct. 1918		Reinforcement 1 O.R.	M.E.
	7 Oct. 1918		Bde moves forward to positions occupied on 4th Oct. in Q.27.a.9.c.	M.E.
	8th Oct 1918		Zero hour 4.30 am. Bde. fire a creeping barrage in support of an attack on SERANVILLERS. Attack successful. Zero hour 6.0 p.m. Bde fire flank defensive barrage in support of attack by Divs. on our left on FORENVILLE and NIERGNIES	M.E. M.E. ##
	9th Oct 1918		Zero hour 5.20 am Bde. fire creeping barrage in support of an attack on WAMBAIX. Attack successful. Midday Bde. moves forward via. CRÈVECOEURT-sur-L'ESCAUT, SERANVILLERS, la TARGETTE, WAMBAIX to positions in H.18.a.5.e. (Sheet 57B.N.W.) due S. of CATTENIÈRES. Killed in Action 1 O.R. Died from wounds 1 O.R.	M.E. M.E. M.C.

Army Form C. 2118.

WAR DIARY
or
INTELLIGENCE SUMMARY.   310 Bde. R.F.A.
(Erase heading not required.)

Instructions regarding War Diaries and Intelligence Summaries are contained in F. S. Regs., Part II. and the Staff Manual respectively. Title pages will be prepared in manuscript.

Place	Date	Hour	Summary of Events and Information	Remarks and references to Appendices
	10th Oct 1918		A.Bty. move forward at 7.0 am working in close support of 1st IRISH GUARDS. Remainder of the Bde. move forward at 9.0 am. to the following positions B.Bty. I 3.6.99.60. C.Bty. I 4.a.2.3. D.Bty. C.27.6.4.3. Bde. H.Q. I. Farm at I 3.c.7.4. N.t BEAUVOIS. Bde. engaged such targets as were hampering the immediate advance of the attacking infantry. Died from wounds. I.O.R.	DMc DMc DMc DMc
	11th Oct 1918.		Bde is in Reserve. 10.0am orders are received to occupy positions in C.5 & 11. N. of St HILAIRE-LES-CAMBRAI, but order is cancelled whilst batteries are moving up. Bde take up a 'position-in-readiness' at REVILLERS C 22 c&d. Bde H.Q. move to St HILAIRE-LES-CAMBRAI. 4.0 p.m. Btys move forward and come into action in C 10.d. W.of ST HILAIRE.	DMc DMc DMc DMc

Army Form C. 2118.

WAR DIARY
or
INTELLIGENCE SUMMARY.

310 Bde R.F.A.

(Erase heading not required.)

Instructions regarding War Diaries and Intelligence Summaries are contained in F.S. Regs., Part II. and the Staff Manual respectively. Title pages will be prepared in manuscript.

Place	Date	Hour	Summary of Events and Information	Remarks and references to Appendices
	12th Oct.1918	4.0 p.m.	At 4.0 p.m. Batteries move forward to positions in D.2.c.(Sheet 57B N.E.) E. of St HILAIRE.	JAC
	13th Oct.18		Between 2.0 p.m. & 4.0 p.m. Bde. fire 1100 rounds into Squares V.18.c & d, & W.13 a & c.	JAC
	14th Oct 1918		Bde withdraw to their Wagon Lines at BÉVILLERS after dusk for four day rest.	JAC
	18th Oct.1918		Bde come into action in their former positions in D.2.c. Bde H.Q. move to D.13.a.75.40.	JAC
	20th Oct 1918	2.0 am	Zero hour 2.0 am Bde fire a creeping shrapnel barrage over SOLESMES from its S.W. to its N.E. outskirts in support of an attack by 62nd Div. All objectives were gained.	JAC
		5.0 am	Btys move forward to positions in D.4.d.	JAC

WAR DIARY
or
INTELLIGENCE SUMMARY.

310 Bde. R.F.A.

Army Form C. 2118.

Place	Date	Hour	Summary of Events and Information	Remarks and references to Appendices
	20th Oct 1918 (contd)	5.20 p.m.	Bde. fire S.O.S. in response to S.O.S. rockets from front line. No hostile attack develops.	
	21st Oct 1918		O.C's Btys reconoiter positions on the eastern outskirts of ST PYTHON.	
	22nd Oct 1918		B.C's reconoitre positions in W.20.a & W.26.b. (Sheet 51A S.E.) During the evening one section of C Bty under command of Lt S.N. CASEY move to a position in readiness on the eastern outskirts of ST PYTHON.	
	23rd Oct 1918	Zero hour 3.20 a.m.	Bde. fire creeping barrage in support of 6 a.m. attack on VERTAIN. 6.0 a.m. Bde. move forward to positions in W.20.c. & W.26.a. 2.26 p.m. Bde fire creeping barrage in support of an attack on ESCARMAIN	

WAR DIARY or INTELLIGENCE SUMMARY

Army Form C. 2118.

310 Bde @ R.F.A.

Place	Date	Hour	Summary of Events and Information	Remarks and references to Appendices
	23rd Oct. 1918 (contd)		During the day the Section of C Bty under Lt. P.N.CASEY. Moves up in close support of 1st Infantry.	JMC
	24th Oct 1918	6 a.m.	Bde. move up to position in readiness in VERTAIN.	JMC
		8.30 a.m.	Bde. move forward to position in readiness in ESCARMAIN.	
		9.30 a.m.	A Bty. comes into action at W.5.L.8.8.(Sheet 51ᴬ S.E.) E. of ESCARMAIN, B Bty in R.25.a., C&D Btys remain in position in readiness. At-dusk C&D Btys come into action in W.5.a. E. of ESCARMAIN.	JMC
	25th Oct 1918		During the morning C&D Btys move forward to positions in R.25.a. During the afternoon C&D Btys sent a section to R.13.d. under the command of Lt. J. Rew. & Lt HAYDOCK resp. A Bty remaining in position in readiness at ESCARMAIN.	
	26th Oct 1918	7.0 a.m.	At 7.0 am All Btys withdrawn to 15th W.L. at ESCARMAIN & from 12th march to QUIEVY to rest & refit.	
	27th to 31st Oct 1918		Bde remain at QUIEVY.	

C W Lly
Major Comdg 310 Bde R.F.A.

Secret

Original

War Diary
of
310th Brigade R.F.A.

Volume XXIII

From 1st November 1918
To 30th November 1918

WAR DIARY
INTELLIGENCE SUMMARY

310 Bde RFA. Army Form C. 2118.

Place	Date	Hour	Summary of Events and Information	Remarks and references to Appendices
	1st Nov.18.		Bde. in rest at QUIÉVY	ME
	2nd Nov.		H.Q. A/B +D batteries move to ESCARMAIN, C By to VERTAIN	ME
	3rd Nov.		After dark batteries move into positions in action N. of RUESNES	ME
	4th Nov.		Zero hour 6.0 a.m. Bde. fire creeping barrage in support of attack on ground N. of LE QUESNOY. During morning Btys advance to positions N. of LE QUESNOY. 2 O.R. Killed in action — 14 wounded.	ME
	5th Nov.		Bde. advance to positions in readiness in Nen. end of MORMAL FOREST. During the evening A+B Btys come into action S.E. of GIMMEGNIES.	ME

ORIGINAL

310 Bde R.F.A.

Army Form C. 2118.

WAR DIARY
INTELLIGENCE SUMMARY.
(Erase heading not required.)

Place	Date	Hour	Summary of Events and Information	Remarks and references to Appendices
	6th Nov. 1918		Morning. Bde. advanced to position in readiness S.E. of OBIES. 1 Gun in to action at night fall. 2 officers wounded.	
	7th Nov. 1918		Bde. fired barrage in support of attack on ground E. of COURTON. Afternoon. Bde. advanced to position in the eastern outskirts of COURTON.	
	8th Nov.		Bde. fired creeping barrage in support of attack on NEUF MESNIL in the morning. Evening. Btys. withdrawn to their W.L. at OBIES.	
	9th Nov.		Bde. in reserve in vicinity of Obies.	
	10th Nov.		Morning. Bde. advanced to NEUF MESNIL. 11.00 Am. Hostilities cease.	

ORIGINAL

310 Bde RFA Army Form C. 2118.

WAR DIARY

INTELLIGENCE SUMMARY.

(Erase heading not required.)

Place	Date	Hour	Summary of Events and Information	Remarks and references to Appendices
	11th-13th Nov.		Bde at NEUF MESNIL. Reinforcements arrived 13th and 2 on 14th.	JHE
	16th Nov.		Bde. march to ROUSIES. 316 Reinforcements arrived	JHE
	19th Nov.		Bde. march to FONTAIN VALMONT.	JHE
	20th Nov.		Bde. march to THY-LE-CHATEAU.	JHE
	24th Nov.		Bde. march to GERPINNES.	JHE
	25th Nov.		Bde. march to ERMETON-sur-BIERT.	JHE
	26th Nov.		Bde. march to Abbey MAREDSOUS	JHE

ORIGINAL

310 Bde. RFA

Army Form C. 2118.

WAR DIARY
INTELLIGENCE SUMMARY.
(Erase heading not required.)

Place	Date	Hour	Summary of Events and Information	Remarks and references to Appendices
	27th Nov 1918		Bde. march through DINANT. H.Q. & D Btys to LOYERS, A Bty to LISOGNE, B Bty to THYNES.	
	28th Nov		Bde. return to LOYERS & LISOGNE, THYNES are...	

WAR DIARY.
Original 310 Bde R.F.A.

1st Decr to 31st Decr 1918

Vol XXIV

WAR DIARY or INTELLIGENCE SUMMARY

Army Form C. 2118.

310 Bde. R.F.A.

Original

Place	Date	Hour	Summary of Events and Information	Remarks and references to Appendices
	Dec 1st–9th 1918		Brigade remains at LOYERS near DINANT.	Me.
	" 3rd		1 Reinforcement arrived (N.O.).	
	Dec 10th 1918		Bde. marches to LEIGNON.	Me.
	Dec 11th 1918		Bde continues march – HQ. to CHANTRAINE, A & E Btys to BUZIN B & D Btys to FAILON.	Me.
	Dec 12th 1918		H.Q. B & D Btys march to OEQUIER, A & E Btys to VERVOX.	Me.
	Dec 13th 1918		Bde. marches to XHORIS	Me.

Original

WAR DIARY
or
INTELLIGENCE SUMMARY. 310 Bde R.F.A.

Army Form C. 2118.

Place	Date	Hour	Summary of Events and Information	Remarks and references to Appendices
	14th Dec. 1918		Bde. continues march. - HQ & C Bty to NOUVILLE A&B Btys to CHEVRON. D Bty to OUFFNY.	MC
	16 Dec 1918		Bde. marches to BASSE-BODEUX, Bde HQ billets in HAUTE BODEUX	MC
	17 Dec 1918		Bde marches over German frontier to WEISMES	MC
	24th Dec 1918		Bde marches to ELSENBORN LAGER.	MC

Army Form C. 2118.

WAR DIARY
or
Original INTELLIGENCE SUMMARY. 310 Bde R.F.A.
(Erase heading not required.)

Place	Date	Hour	Summary of Events and Information	Remarks and references to Appendices
	22nd Dec 1918		H.Q. A B & D Btys marched to MÜTZENICH, C Bty to KONZEN.	MC
	23rd Dec 1918		Bde. marched to DREIBORN	MC
	25 Dec 1918		Bde. marched to GEMUND.	MC
	25th Dec 1918		1 O.R. Reinforcement received	MC
	30th Dec 1918		4 O.R. " "	MC
	26–31st Dec 1918		Bde remains at GEMUND.	MC

WAR DIARY
or
INTELLIGENCE SUMMARY.

3/10 BDE R.F.A. Army Form C. 2118.

JANUARY 98 25

Place	Date	Hour	Summary of Events and Information	Remarks and references to Appendices
	1st–31st Jan 1919.		Bde stationed at GEMÜND.	nil
	4th Jan		Transferred to U.K. for dispersal — 2 others Ranks	
	5th		— 1 — 1 — 1	Seven
	6th		— 1 — 4 — 1	
	9th		— 3 — 1 —	All were ready for O.R.'s since OM

"Original"

310 BRIGADE. R.F.A.

VI 26

WAR DIARY
or
INTELLIGENCE SUMMARY.
(Erase heading not required.)

Army Form C. 2118.

Place	Date	Hour	Summary of Events and Information	Remarks and references to Appendices
1-26 Feb			Brigade stationed at GEMÜND. NMS	
3 Feb.			Transferred to U.K. for disposal – 2 other ranks	NMS
4"			– 1 –	NMS
6"			– 2 –	NMS
7"			– 1 –	NMS
8"			– 2 –	NMS
9"			– 1 –	NMS
15"			– 2 officers –	NMS

McFadden Capt

Original.

14th I.

310th BDE. RFA.

WAR DIARY

VOL D.27

Confidential.

WAR DIARY
or
INTELLIGENCE SUMMARY.

310 BRIGADE R.F.A.

Army Form C. 2118.

Place	Date	Hour	Summary of Events and Information	Remarks and references to Appendices
	1 - 31st March		Brigade stationed at GEMÜND.	ESS
	28th + 29th		2 Officers & reinforcements received. 63 O.R.o	ESS

E S Shrok
Lieut. Colonel.
Comdg. 310th Field Artillery Brigade.

Army Form C. 2118.

WAR DIARY
or
INTELLIGENCE SUMMARY.

(Erase heading not required.)

Instructions regarding War Diaries and Intelligence Summaries are contained in F. S. Regs., Part II. and the Staff Manual respectively. Title pages will be prepared in manuscript.

310th BRIGADE R.F.A. - MAY 1919 -

Place	Date	Hour	Summary of Events and Information	Remarks and references to Appendices
GEMUND.	1st to 10th		Demobilisation proceeded and new drafts arrived, so that by 10th May the Brigade was complete with retainable men. These proved to be very raw, and vigorous training was begun. Shortage of experienced N.C.O's proved a difficulty.	
VLATTEN.	10th.		On this day Brigade moved from GEMUND to new area and were billeted as follows;- Headquarters and "B"/310 at VLATTEN; C/310 at WOLLERSHEIM; and A/310 at EMBKEN. D/310 remained at the BARRACKS, DUREN.	
do	13th.		D/310 with troops of the DUREN garrison were inspected by the Commander in Chief, Army of Rhine, who expressed his appreciation of the good turn out.	
do	10th to 31st.		Batteries settled down in their new area. Section Training commenced. Brigade Education School instituted. Recreation hampered by shortage of Summer Sport Kit which was ordered from England.	
do	26th		Major-General Sir D. Campbell, G.O.C., Highland Division, inspected the Brigade during training.	

3rd June 1919.

[signature]

Lieut-Col. R.F.A.,
Commanding 310th Brigade R.F.A.

Confidential.

WAR DIARY

of

310 Brigade R.F.A.

From 1/8/19.   To. 30/8/19.

Army Form C. 2118.

WAR DIARY
or
INTELLIGENCE SUMMARY.

(Erase heading not required.)

Instructions regarding War Diaries and Intelligence Summaries are contained in F. S. Regs., Part II. and the Staff Manual respectively. Title pages will be prepared in manuscript.

Place	Date	Hour	Summary of Events and Information	Remarks and references to Appendices
VLATTEN.	June 1919		Training has continued vigorously throughout the month.	
			Shortage of experienced N.C.Os is still proving a difficulty.	
			Recreation has been hampered by the poor weather conditions.	
	15.7.19.			

[signature]

Lieut. Col, R.F.A.
Commanding 310th Brigade, R. F. A.

ORIGINAL

Army Form C. 2118.

WAR DIARY
or
INTELLIGENCE SUMMARY.
(Erase heading not required.)

310 Bde R.F.A.

WAR DIARY

310 Bde R.F.A.

July 1919

(Volume)

Army Form C. 2118.

WAR DIARY
or
INTELLIGENCE SUMMARY.
(Erase heading not required.)

Instructions regarding War Diaries and Intelligence Summaries are contained in F. S. Regs., Part II. and the Staff Manual respectively. Title pages will be prepared in manuscript.

Place	Date	Hour	Summary of Events and Information	Remarks and references to Appendices
	JULY 1919.		310th BRIGADE, R. F. A.	
VLATTEN.	10th		Training proceeded during the month.	
			On this day 7 Officers of the Brigade and one Section of A/310 proceeded to the Artillery Range at ELSENBORN CAMP to calibrate guns equipped with the 18-pdr Mark IV and to train Officers in the handling of the new equipment.	
			This party returned on the 18th July.	
			Recreational Training has been satisfactorily carried out during the month.	

3.8.19.

Lieut-Colonel, R.F.A.
Commanding 310th Brigade, R. F. A.

Hyland 62 Siv

Confidential

War Diary
of
310th Bde. R.F.A.

From Aug 1st 1919.   To Aug 31st 1919.

Army Form C. 2118.

WAR DIARY
or
INTELLIGENCE SUMMARY.
(Erase heading not required.)

Instructions regarding War Diaries and Intelligence Summaries are contained in F. S. Regs., Part II. and the Staff Manual respectively. Title pages will be prepared in manuscript.

Place	Date	Hour	Summary of Events and Information	Remarks and references to Appendices
VLATTEN. GERMANY.	1 to 13.		Instructions having been received for the Highland Divisional Artillery to proceed to England, the Unit's Guns and Stores were despatched to Ordnance DUREN, and the horses were transhipped to England.	
			The Brigade left VLATTEN on the 13th of August, and arrived in HEYTESBURY CAMP, WILTSHIRE on the night of the 15th.	
HEYTESBURY. WILTSHIRE.	16 to 31.		On arrival permission was granted for 50% of the personnel of the Brigade to proceed on 14 days leave and this party left on 18th.	
			216 Horses for the Brigade arrived from the Remount Depot, Shirehampton on the 27th.	
			During the period 16th to 31st, 125 O.Rs were despatched for demobilisation in accordance with Army Orders Nos 292 and 293.	

HEYTESBURY.
Wiltshire.
1.9.1919.

M.H. Siddons Capt
for Major R.F.A.,
Commanding 51th Brigade R.F.A.

311 BDE RFA
Became

311 ARMY FIELD ARTILLERY BDE
_____

1 ARMY
_____

www.ingramcontent.com/pod-product-compliance
Lightning Source LLC
Chambersburg PA
CBHW081429160426
43193CB00013B/2234